1 1 APR 20 ☑ KT-574-532

2 4 JUL 2018

... award winning YES Change
(www.yesindeed.com) and the founder of the extreme sports media company Black Diamond Films (www.blackdiamond.co.uk).

As a professional actor he performed in Hollywood films, in London's West End theatres, on national and international television and as part of the BBC's improvisation team performing to live audiences of 15 million people. He also won an Olivier Award for his work with the Royal Opera House.

He launched his first business, Black Diamond Films, at the age of 21, marketing and distributing extreme sports films. Black Diamond became the leading distributor of specialist film in Europe within four years. He sold out of Black Diamond and began YES, an award-winning consultancy designing seminars and change programmes for public- and private-sector clients.

He has designed and delivered seminars and change programmes for public- and private-sector clients for over 20 years. He has personally trained over 200,000 people in the areas of communication, creativity, collaboration and Purposeful leadership. His style is interactive and engaging, leaning on storytelling, comedy and improvisation to develop accelerated learning and build new habits of effectiveness. Recently he has specialized in pioneering new forms of learning using a wide variety of media, interactive theatre, online learning and "serious play". He is currently advising the European Union (EU) on change strategies.

C334145246

The 7 Questions to Find Your Purpose

Richard Jacobs

WATKINS

Sharing Wisdom Since
1893

This edition first published in the UK and USA 2017 by

Watkins, an imprint of Watkins Media Limited

19 Cecil Court

London WC2N 4EZ

enquiries@watkinspublishing.com

Design and typography copyright © Watkins Media Limited 2017

Text copyright © Richard Jacobs 2017

Richard Jacobs has asserted his right under the Copyright, Designs and Patents Act 1988 to be identified as the author of this work.

All rights reserved.

No part of this book may be reproduced or utilized in any form or by any means, electronic or mechanical, without prior permission in writing from the Publishers.

1 3 5 7 9 10 8 6 4 2

Designed and typeset by JCS Publishing Services Ltd

Printed and bound in the United Kingdom by CPI Group (UK) Ltd, Croydon CR0 4YY

A CIP record for this book is available from the British Library

ISBN: 978-1-78678-113-0

www.watkinspublishing.com

Contents

Acknowledgements

I would like to thank my wife Kalinka for her irrepressible passion for self-discovery and personal evolution; for her guidance, support, wisdom and love; for her refusal to entertain anything other than authenticity; for her tenacity, for excellence and her embodiment of elegance. She also did all the illustrations for the book. Thank you.

I would like to thank my children Zac and Keera for reinventing the world, for their radiance and brightness and for teaching me every day.

I would like to thank and acknowledge all the people who have come through my seminars. It is through them that anything I have of value to offer was forged, refined, tested and packaged. A roomful of people is intelligent and I have been fortunate enough to stand at the front of many thousands of rooms. Thank you for your willingness and kindness.

I would like to thank Jo and all the team at Watkins for making this book happen. I am deeply grateful in continuously unfolding ways.

Lastly, I would like to bow deeply to the Purposeful people who have made films, music, discoveries and world-changing speeches; who have stood for their principles, been the voices of generations and who have echoed a timeless voice through the idioms of the ages.

You are my inspiration.

Introduction

What's the meaning of life? Anybody? Twenty words or less please. Is it love? Spiritual enlightenment? Just having fun? This is not a new question. For thousands of years people have been postulating theories. Some have gone to war, needing to prove that they are right... "We know the meaning of life, so we're going to end yours as a way of proving it." Who's got the answer? Nobody? Everybody? Maybe there is no answer. What if the meaning of life is the meaning *you* find in *your* life. If that's the case, then everybody's right; however, they are only right about themselves. They have no idea about what's right for anybody else.

Neither do I.

You do, though. You know exactly what's right for you. You know what gives your life Purpose and meaning. You know what's most important to you. You know what most inspires you and in the deepest recesses of your mind the places that surface when you're looking out of the window of a moving train and your mind drifts into the place between imagination and knowledge. For a fleeting moment everything falls into place. There is a gentle, deep breath and an order to the world takes shape. An order that is only meant for you. It's accompanied by a quiet knowing, a feeling of recognition and understanding ... and then a baby cries, or the phone pings, a food trolley selling imitation sandwiches rolls past your seat and the reverie ends. Real life seems to take over and the sumptuous clarity of the window-gazing silence seems to fade as if that were the dream and the sandwich trolley were real life.

We can all get to these places, but for most people it happens by accident – or at least in an ad hoc fashion. What we need is a sure-fire way to access this quality of contemplation. The Internet has so much information, it would be impossible to navigate without a search engine. The same is true for the "innernet". We need search engines. And these come in the form of questions.

Einstein said, "It's not that I'm so smart, I just stay with problems longer." When we focus our attention and go progressively deeper we can find most of the answers we seek. The question is, how do we do this? Do we need to spend years sitting on a mountain top, talking to gurus and spiritual teachers and drinking magical potions? Don't get me wrong, all that stuff's great. I love it. But do we need it? Our Purpose, our sense of meaning, is innate. It could not be our Purpose otherwise. We simply need a way that makes it easy to go inwards and find the source.

I grew up an Indiana Jones fan. When I watched him go into a cave or a temple and face a thousand challenges it always struck me how easy it was for the people who followed him. All they had to do was follow in his footsteps and they would surely avoid the traps. The good news is that many thousands have trodden the seven footsteps you are about to take. Their journeys have refined and simplified the route, avoiding the common pitfalls of the conscious mind, the misplaced modesties, the scars of teachers and the unfulfilled expectations of youth. This book is designed as a unique search engine that will reveal to you what you already know but may never have named. At its heart are seven questions, the structure, style and content of which are designed to help you stay long enough to find and name your Purpose. For most people about an hour and a half is enough. Following the seven questions, the book is devoted to helping you to mine the riches of your answers as well as experiments to help your Purpose come off the page and into your life, moment by moment, action by action.

Throughout the book there are stories about people who have gone through the process, and examples from workshops and seminars I have given in the corporate world.

I do a lot of work with large organizations to trigger meaningful behavioural change. My specialism is scaleable programmes working with large groups of people. In other words, training and change that lead people to fundamentally shift their mindsets and behaviours so that they are more effective, more fulfilled and more aligned with each other. Sometimes this is for 500 people in one office, sometimes it's for 70,000 people in 80 countries.

A lot of the formative work described in this book has taken place in the corporate environment and with non-governmental organizations (NGOs) and government. This has proved to be a unique design brief. It requires an approach that cuts out all the fat, the waffle and the hope, and helps create new and more effective ways of engaging people. The material has been influenced in two key ways:

People coming to a work seminar have not paid or, for the most part, chosen to be there. This means that the material needs to strike a chord with them, regardless of any personal reticence, office politics or the fact that while they are sitting in a chair listening to me another ten emails have hit their inbox. The material needs to be incisive and resilient.

Organizations want measureable results. "I feel good" or "I've got a better idea of what works for me" does not cut it in the corporate world. My clients range from Coca-Cola, Google and Unilever, to the European Union (EU), NGOs and charities. They need to know that the precious time of their people has been well spent and that means being able to measure the difference an intervention makes. Time is money, tick tock. A seminar needs to have a "before" and "after" – meaning that people are fundamentally different after having embarked on such a course.

My background is in acting in theatre, film, television and improvisation. I started designing and delivering seminars when I was 25. I have been fortunate enough to train over 200,000 people and make media for many hundreds of thousands more. I have designed a multitude of culture change programmes and worked with organizations at the head of the food chain, such as NGOs, charities, refugee groups and schools. I have collaborated with people in 30 languages and 80 countries. I think in the end, we're all fundamentally the same. We all want peace, loving relationships, a sense of meaning and truth in our lives, and to feel in our autumn years that the world is somehow richer for our presence. So where does this sense of fulfilment come from? And do we have to wait until it's nearly all over before we realize what is truly important to us?

Is it lodged in the glossy magazine images of success and the glitterati stories showing the lifestyles of the rich and famous iconized as the pinnacle of aspiration? Isn't it curious how many of those people suffer from depression, addiction or an inability to hold down long-term, meaningful relationships? Maybe the truth of fulfilment is much more dynamic, profoundly energized and free.

7 Questions to Find Your Purpose helps you to define and live according to what is most important to you. Purpose is a focus, an intent. This process asks you: What do you intend to give to the world? Do you wish to leave this planet with things untried, undone and unsaid? In our heart of hearts, each of us wants to live life deeply in integrity with who we are and our highest vision of the world. Every time we go against this deep sense of knowing and "rightness" we eat away at our own energy source and we become compromised human beings ... someone who has settled for less than their best, who has become jaded, tired and believing more in limitation than in possibility.

Purpose is the acupuncture point of integrity. When we live Purposefully our values and our highest beliefs, everything that is meaningful to us, come into alignment and we become the expression of the best part of ourselves.

A friend of mine, who eventually died of AIDS, told me the following story: back in the days when it took six weeks to get the results of an AIDS test, a man was convinced that he had contracted the virus because one of his previous partners was HIV positive. While he waited, he made lists of all the things he wanted to do with his life: the places he would go, the people he would meet, and those with whom he would make amends. When the day of his results came he was clear about what he wanted to do. It turned out that he had not contracted HIV. He was overjoyed and had his friends round to celebrate. Over dinner he produced his lists and was just about to burn them over the candles when someone asked him what he was doing.

"I'm burning my lists. I'm going to live now. I don't need them any more."

"But now you know what you want out of life," his friend exclaimed.

"Yes," he replied.

"Then why not live it? If you were going to die in a year you would have lived everything on that list. Now that you have 60 years left you may as well spend your whole life living what you want. That is the most valuable list you could have."

I was very inspired by the story. What was really important to people when they faced the end of their life? The answers seemed clear: that they had lived according to their core values, meaning how much love had they given and received in their life. They also wanted to feel somehow that the world was richer for their presence. Don't we all want that? What would we do if only we gave ourselves the time and authority? How much of what we truly wish for ourselves do we pursue? And do we have to be on our deathbeds to know what's important?

Years ago when my children were very young they moved from a private school near us to the local school. They are twins and so they joined the same class. In the new school they had a part of the day called "choosing", when each child could choose how he or she wanted to explore the lesson they were learning. For example, if they were learning about travel, they could go to a table and make passports out of cardboard, make airplanes out of Lego, draw pictures and so on.

At the first "choosing" session my daughter happily went off to the art table because she loves to draw and paint, while my son stood in the centre of the room and didn't know what to do. He didn't know how to choose. I was horrified when I found out. I realized that the expensive private school turned out very "correct", nicely behaved kids who had no idea how to make choices for themselves because they were always told what to do. What happens if this carries on for a few more years or all through school? Perhaps by then the idea of being in touch with our true choices is so alien to us that we just don't know how to do it any more and we become permanently compromised.

How many of us have actually exercised our ability to choose? Most of us have had others do our choosing for us – schools, subjects, what others think is best for us, advice on career choices, partners and so on. What are the criteria we have chosen in accordance with up until now? Other people's. Other people's criteria, which they cut and pasted from their peers. Groundhog Day.

It took my son six weeks to learn how to choose what he really wanted to do. Now, of course, it's completely natural again.

When we've decided to choose our lives as opposed to living by default, what is it that sponsors and guides those choices? Knowing and living your Purpose is knowing yourself, your best self. It is this that brings our best life to fruition. What else could? To cook a really satisfying meal you have to know what you like. To live a life that is an exalted expression of our Purpose, our values, and expressed through the media of our gifts, talents and abilities, we have to know what these things are. How many of us have the luxury of sitting on a Tibetan mountain-top in deep meditation until epiphany strikes? What if we didn't need to? What if we already know our Purpose in life? In a way, how could we not? If you sit very still and try and focus on feeling your spine, can you feel it? For most of us, unless it's painful, the answer is "no". Does that mean our spine is not there? Of course not. We simply have to move or exercise it to feel it again. It's the same with Purpose. It's there. It's inside us. How could it not be? We simply have to have a way to focus on it and then to exercise it.

The first chapter of the book, called Beginnings, outlines what Purpose is and isn't, and reveals how we can discover – by asking the right questions – what is most important to us. We can draw upon our creative imagination and harness our subconscious to unearth the inner "diamond" of Purpose. Beginnings concludes by explaining the "YES" factor, and how that will equip you with the necessary tool to answer key questions. The second chapter of the book explores the Seven Questions system, which is a sophisticated and foolproof way of googling the unconscious so that we can know, fundamentally, what Purpose we serve in life. The answers reveal a world of discovery, which is examined in depth. The third chapter, Purpose at Work, is about practical application: how we can apply Purpose in our lives, which is explored in work-related scenarios, with a particular focus on six key themes. The fourth chapter, Purpose in Action, is about the transformation of our lives more broadly and outlines the key principles of Purpose that enable radical change to happen.

Spread throughout the book are "experiments" and exercises, which are a variety of diverse ways you can explore the application of the principles and ideas. These experiments and exercises are designed to be fun, interesting and with a hint of adventure.

1

Beginnings

The first course I designed was "Presentation Skills and Public Speaking". It came about because I was due to deliver a training programme for a large organization. The night before, I was leafing through the trainer's manual and I thought: "This is nonsense. I may not know much about training but I know a thing or two about being on stage and if I translated what I'm reading here to there, people would throw things at me." However, I needed the work and wanted to deliver it. The solution was to write my own course. I jotted down some notes, literally on the back of an envelope – about 20 minutes of prep. The course was a huge success. I kept on delivering it and refining it and became the top-rated trainer of the company. It took me seven years to understand what I had written in those 20 minutes.

I have been delivering this course in different forms for years. I noticed that people were fixated on "saying the right words" as opposed to saying what they meant. This is something that distinguishes amateur actors from professionals. So many amateurs think about how to say a line, whereas a professional focuses on why they say a line. I would constantly ask people, "What do you mean?"

"This is what I think I need to say..."

"OK... but what do you mean? What do you mean? What do you mean?"

Eventually they would tell me. And when they spoke from a place of meaning, all the lights came on. They were present, they spoke compellingly, simply and one could not help but be convinced. In short, they became the best part of themselves. It started to occur to me then: if this is what happens to a person when they start to speak from a place of meaning, what would happen to them if they started *living* from a place of meaning?

Around this time a call came in asking me if I would deliver a workshop for a major architectural firm in Washington, DC. I was very excited. It was the first time I was being flown across the world by a client. It was a wonderful opportunity and a very different session to the ones I had been used to delivering. I had been working with the UK branch of the firm for several years, delivering my communication programme. That had been very successful and the word had got back to the "president", hence the call.

The brief was to focus the worst-performing department, to unite the predominant players and inject new life into a tired and demoralized team. I didn't realize it at the time but this was a pivotal session. Behind the scenes it was clear that this was their last chance. Either they pulled things out of the bag or the whole department would be canned and several hundred people made redundant. Neither I nor the rest of the team knew anything about this at that stage; however, people must have been feeling the pressure somewhat because we had lots of conference calls leading up to the event.

I wasn't used to this. My speciality had been "impro training", which is code for minimal preparation and a preference for searching out the inspiration in the moment when it was required. Suddenly I was being asked to prepare, which felt a bit like homework. In the conference calls I was being asked questions like: "What are your plans?" "What are you going to take us through to unify the group, bring us to the clarity and focus we need for the forthcoming year?" "How can we follow up?" These, of course, are normal questions and it would now feel strange to run a major event without having these conversations. At the time, however, it was all new to me. I hadn't run an event of this type – at director-level in a highly politicized environment. I was a bit out of my depth.

I found that I knew the answers to their questions as they came out. The words would form in my mouth a fraction of a second before the thought took shape. I was a grateful witness to a becoming. I only realized the wisdom of what I was saying long after the event.

Voice one: "What are you going to do to unify the group?"

Me, *trying to buy some time*: "How many people will be there?"

Voice two: "50."

Me: "How will you know that you got there?" *Thinking, How will I know that we got there?*

Voice one: "That's a good question."

Me, *thinking, Phew...*

Voices one, two and three: "Hmmm. We'll feel it. There's a quality isn't there? Our results actually. We'll be more successful and get there faster."

General murmurs of agreement.

Me, *thinking, What's the ultimate in unity? What does that feel like? It's a bit like my water polo team – everyone played a different position and contributed to the whole. All different, same focus and we were unstoppable.* "OK, Purpose. We'll do a section where we determine your collective purpose. It must be something that everyone buys into, something they are prepared to give themselves to completely. They must love it and it must serve the business."

Voice one: "That sound terrific. Can you put that down on paper for us and let's speak again in a few days."

Me: "OK fine." *Thinking, What!?* "Let's speak then."

In the next few days, I had lots of conversations with my wife. She has this extremely annoying but amazingly inspirational habit of asking questions that I don't know the answers to and really need to know the answers to:

Kalinka: "So how are you going to get to Purpose?"

Me: "We'll have a discussion. I'll ask them questions."

Kalinka: "What are you going to ask them?"

Me, *fumbling*: "All sorts of stuff."

Kalinka: "Like what?"

Me, *starting to pace now*: (Now I realize I think much better when I move. Thank you Sir Ken Robinson's TED Talk "Do schools kill creativity?") "I'll need to ask them about their values... see where they're aligned."

Kalinka: "What about the motivation part?"

Me: "Well they must love it. I'm going to ask them questions to help them connect with what it is in the work that most ignites them. What would they ultimately love their work to serve."

Kalinka: "That's good but... How do you know that they're going to be authentic in their answers?"

Me: "I'm sure I'll know. *Actually, I'm not sure I'll know at all.*"

Kalinka: "You said that they were highly politicized. That means they're going to try to impress the boss. They'll say what they think others want to hear."

Me: "Yes, yes."

Kalinka: "So what're you going to do?"

Me: "I'm thinking... thinking... YES. I'll ask them how much it says 'YES' to them out of ten?"

Kalinka: "And..."

Me: "And make a rule that we only action eights and above. We all have to be eight, nine or ten. We'll call it the 'YES factor'."

Kalinka: "The 'YES factor', I like it."

Me, *very proud and a bit relieved*: "Thank you."

Silence.

Kalinka: "How are you going to introduce it?"

Me, *Oh God...*

Fortunately, a few days later, our neighbour Dani (http://themeditationteacher.net), one of the brightest stars in the firmament, showed us a film about why geese fly in V formation. It said:

"As each goose flaps its wings, it creates an updraught for the bird behind it."

"Through flying in this formation, they collectively achieve 71 per cent extra distance with the same effort as flying alone, which allows them to traverse the Atlantic."

"The lead goose rotates every so often so they can rest and each goose gets a turn. If one goose is ill or tired, two stop with it so that they can create a mini V and catch up with the rest."

"Throughout the flight the geese 'honk' constantly, encouraging each other and uniting the flock."

"This is what allows geese to live the lifestyle they do... travelling around the world enjoying an endless summer."

It was a perfect model of collaboration, compassion and connection. The Purpose was an endless summer – the good life. Their V equates to an alignment of values. The encouragement and insistence that everyone is on the same journey equates to community and connection... the culture of the department.

Geese have brains the size of olives. If they could do it...

So that's exactly what we did. Geese became the iconic metaphor. I wrote a series of questions asking about people's values, their gifts, the contribution they would be most inspired to make and I checked every response with the "YES factor". They had to know they had chosen the same thing – eight, nine or ten out of ten.

I ended up designing a lot of that workshop "on the spot"... changing my questions, finding more creative ways of asking people's views on things. For example, I realized that when I asked a group "What do you think of 'x'?", they would give me a stilted and manicured response.

However, if I asked them "If we could look inside everybody's head in the organization and find out what they thought about 'x', what do you think they would say?" The responses came thick and fast. People were fluid and committed in their speech. They hit the same patterns I had witnessed so many times in my presentation skills training (www. yesindeed.com – look at online courses) when people spoke from their centre – from their place of power and confidence. They didn't know what people really thought, they were projecting their own thoughts onto others and found it much easier to talk from this perspective. I started to see the power of "what if". People could let go of themselves, stop being "correct" and let loose what they really thought and felt.

This, combined with genuine answers and then confirmed by the "YES factor" ("How much does this say YES to you out of ten – only action eights and above"), saved so much time. Knowing that we all wanted to get above an eight meant that we didn't have to talk about people's sixes and sevens. Being right and making sure that other people bought into our point of view was no longer on the table, only the number. The only question was: "How can we pop this up to an eight or nine?" In one stroke we had lobotomized internal politics... what Jack Canfield referred to as "the cancer of an organization". People looking after their personal interests regardless of the whole versus people who were authentically eight, nine or ten out of ten are always moving in favour of themselves AND the whole – a much more sustainable and enjoyable status quo. We had put a greater value on higher agreement than on power and influence.

In the year following the workshop that department became seven times more impactful. This was measured by:

- New work and profitability.
- Staff retention.

- The speed at which they were able to complete assignments.
- The level of cooperation between teams and departments.

My conclusions from that event were:

- A roomful of people is intelligent.
- There are more dynamic ways of asking questions.
- You lobotomize politics when you genuinely work for the highest good for all.

This seminar forged the way for a multitude of variations and experiments, the fruits of which you will find in these pages.

What Purpose is...

Your best bit.

Purpose is meaning. What then do we find "meaning-full"?

1. Eight, nine, ten: If you could measure your life experience on a scale of one to ten with ten being "fantastic, great, a rollercoaster, I love life" and one being "I've got a pulse". Purpose is always above an eight.
2. It's inside us: It can't be anywhere else. What gives meaning to each of us is distinct. It can't be found in the external. It must necessarily be within, in our experience of life. Cars, houses, beaches, partners and wine is all great and wonderful, but they are decorations to our lives. They are not in and of themselves meaningful. It is what we bring to them that gives rise to meaningful experience. It is always about how much of ourselves we give which brings out our best and consequently the best in others, on the beaches, sipping the wine.

We treat experience as something passive, as if the taste of food "happens to us" or the film was "entertaining" or "interesting". It's not. It's active. We lean into the present moment, extending ourselves toward it: tasting the food; engaging the characters in a film. Life is the same: we have to extend ourselves into it to experience every morsel. Purposeful people are passionate. All we take with us at the end of our days is our experiences. Where do you want yours to figure on a scale of one to ten?

3. Gotta give: If giving ourselves leads to a fuller experience of life, then giving to others is what triggers our catalogue of abilities. These abilities become the conduits of our expression. And if we indulge and dive deeply into the expression of our abilities, how could that experience be anything other than meaningful? Our Purpose is something we serve. It is, by definition, greater than ourselves.

So here it is... our Purpose is the intersection of our values, our gifts, talents and abilities, and the contribution we are most inspired to make. That crossover point is incandescent. It is the key to your mastery, the open door to your soul and... it makes you relevant.

"Relevant? What do you mean, relevant?"

When we give the best of ourselves to the highest good we suddenly become relevant to the whole. It's as if we intersect with our community, society and the world in a different way, with the inter-face being our talents. It's a perfect system. It's as if the world wakes up and recognizes us. I was delivering training sessions to 12 people at a time, getting excellent results and making a comfortable living. I then discovered Purpose. Almost immediately I was asked (asked!) to design a programme that would trigger a fundamental shift in 10,000 people in a year, requiring me to call on all my experience in theatre as well as combining with that of the training room; from 12 to 10,000 in the blink of an eye.

You become relevant.

What Purpose isn't...

Your job, your possessions, something you must fulfil, your destiny.

Your job

Our Purpose is greater than us. It is a path of expression and exploration. When Mahatma Gandhi became active in South Africa his self-nominated job was "to elevate the status of the Indian community with legal rights and safeguards"; his Purpose, however, was not fulfilled or confined by his job. We might say that his Purpose was "the non-violent emancipation of all peoples" and his actions admirably served this. Seen this way, one's Purpose is the through line and trajectory of what you choose to serve, bring or create.

Purpose isn't your job. It's *also* your job.

You are not defined by what you do.

You are *and* you do.

Your destiny

What is destiny really? It is the journey toward your destination. YOUR destination. You choose it. Sometimes we get a feeling of destiny, as if everything is flowing to this single moment in time and there is such a feeling of "rightness" to it that it must be ordained, given by something or someone bigger than me? Surely?

What if it isn't that at all? What if it's really what we would choose for ourselves if we were living the eight, nine or ten part of ourselves?

Maybe it's that which feels so "right", so compelling, so all-inspiring. Maybe we're just not used to feeling like that. When at school, were you asked, "What's your Purpose?" "OK class, gather round. At some point in your life you're going to make choices about how you want to live, so let's explore your greatest gifts, the ones that are not measured by our curriculum, and the path that will inspire and ignite you beyond words." I don't know about you, but that never happened to me. Neither was I asked it at home, by my friends, in television programmes, in the cinema... anywhere in society, in fact. It wasn't on the cards. How then, could I have had any experience of my eight, nine or ten, except in anything other than an arbitrary fashion – something I could not repeat at will, let alone build my life around.

Destiny is when we are on our way to our highest destination. So in that sense, Purpose is your destiny.

Your relationship

Do we define ourselves by our relationships? I'm a husband, or a wife, or a mother, or a daughter, or a son. Yes, these things give meaning to our lives, but we cannot let other people define who we are. Nobody knows who we are. Not really. We think we know other people perfectly. We don't; but thinking that we do means we make up a million assumptions about them. Most of the time we have no idea if those assumptions are correct, but lacking any other evidence we just assume that they are and carry on. Not knowing but thinking that we do is putting someone "in a box" in our minds. We want and expect them to behave in predictable ways and often get upset when they don't. "That's just not like you!" How do we know? Perhaps if we could see the inner lives of the people we meet we would realize how similar we all are. However, the reality is that we are all infinite variations on a theme. Our uniqueness is our greatest asset and the reason we have the ability to express ourselves. Our value is that distinctiveness. The great erosive collusion of society, however, is that we all try to "fit in". As unfair and inaccurate as it is to box up other people, it is equally unproductive for them to do the same to you. You do not share the same fingerprints, thoughts, laugh, voice, gait or regard as any other human being who has ever lived or who ever will. Not only that, but sometimes when we get married, or become parents or managers, we start "playing a role", unconsciously mirroring those role models and emulating them in the circumstances of our lives. This is something that is so ingrained in us – to repeat the patterns of our parents and teachers – that we have no idea we are doing it. The "role" just seems to fit. With that, though, comes routine – the unmindful repetition of actions for the sake of habit. Have you ever been driving in your car and found yourself taking roads which are familiar patterns instead of driving where you want to go? We all do it in different areas of our lives. These are routines. With that lack of mindfulness we put a part of our aliveness to sleep.

You cannot be defined by a relationship, you can only express yourself in it. What you choose to express, therefore, can be in alignment with your Purpose. We can be a husband and Purposeful, a Purposeful wife, a Purposeful son, a Purposeful manager.

Your definition, if you need one, is through your Purpose, not through a role.

The iceberg

There is no relationship between effort and effectiveness. An aikido master can put an attacker on the floor using two fingers. It's not about effort, it's about leverage.

If you or I were to swim two lengths of a pool we would use much more effort than an Olympic swimmer. The refinement in their style means that they get more done with less energy. Their effectiveness is determined by their technique and the relationship between themselves and the element they are in, rather than through effort alone. It's not the effort, it's the glide.

The mind is like an iceberg. Over 80 per cent of it is beneath the surface. The conscious mind is the bit that we see. The unconscious mind is the rest... the vast majority. To put it another way, your conscious mind is the screen of the computer, the unconscious is the hard drive and interface with the Internet. You need the conscious mind, yes, but it's not where the main action is. We have to start accessing our unconscious, deciphering it and respecting its unique language and style if we are going to delve deeply into our possibility as human beings.

In organizations we change culture through harnessing subculture. In individuals we change our programming via our subconscious. That is where we have to go to seed Purpose.

Harnessing the subconscious exploits the principle that there is no relationship between effort and effectiveness.

Using the conscious mind to access the unconscious. Why? Because the conscious mind is where all our training is. It's hard in the conscious mind to distinguish between what we've been told we want and what we really want. To choose our Purpose we have to be able to make free choices.

In this book we rely heavily on the place where our creativity and intuition overlap. That is the acupuncture point of effortless effectiveness. People sometimes have trouble accepting this principle. They seem to feel that the best way to succeed at things is simply to work hard at them. However, if we had as much sense as geese, we would know that there are ways of using our energy to give us great results and which require very little effort. In their V formation, geese put in 29 per cent effort and get 100 per cent out. If they fly alone, out of integrity with their highest good, they put in 100 per cent effort to get 100 per cent out. We are the same; if you think of your "inner geese" as the collective point around which all your values collect, when we "fly" with our inner geese out of alignment, we are wasting the best part of ourselves. Collectively and individually, when we focus our efforts around a single Purpose, we accomplish our goals faster and with a greater sense of fulfilment and morale. If greater effectiveness and well-being comes from a single point of focus, how can that principle be applied to us all as individuals? How do we get our "inner geese" in order?

I have put together a series of questions appealing to our creative-intuitive mind to help you discover what is most important to you; to reveal your values and what you would be most inspired to give in this lifetime. Our logical mind says how the world ought to be, which is heavily influenced by upbringing, education, the world, our peers and our own quickly drawn judgements about what is right and wrong. Our creative-intuitive mind sees how things could be; and that could be both fantastic and practical. We can watch a film or read a story set in a world where it is totally acceptable for animals to talk, trees to walk and the sky to have friends, yet if someone suggests the possibility of world peace within our lifetime or of having more weekend than week, people reject the possibility. Our creative imagination is free and allows us the possibility of making choices unfettered by our past or the pressures of modern society. Imagination will be the route into our truth. Each question acts as a clue into an ever-deepening inner treasure hunt. As you answer them in honesty and integrity, they unravel their wisdoms and you progress to the next until eventually you discover your "diamond" within... Purpose.

We are repositories of experience. In the end that is all life is – experience. And that experience is determined by the intentions we have and the choices we make in every moment. Purpose is the cohesion of our intentions. Over the time I have worked with my Purpose, I have learned that I am more than my job or the role I play in society. I have learned that as I live and give my values, I become Value-able to the whole. What I do is far less important than the focus and intention that I give to it, *that* becomes my experience of the world and therefore my life. I am not my job, my home, my relationship, my car. Everything I have and everything I am is an extension of me, and the more I live my Purpose the more meaningful my life becomes. I have had plenty of money and I have had none, but in the end it is of little consequence. The only thing that matters is the meaning I give to my life and the quality of my experience. That together is my true richness.

Sharpening the pencil

Pretty soon you're going to be answering the seven questions of Purpose. Below are some principles to "sharpen your pencil" and help you to give the best of yourself to the process.

Answering the questions is a very simple process. Each question acts as a search engine for the subconscious mind, which is best accessed through your imagination. Our imagination is where we are free of limitations and is the fastest place to gain insight and the fundamental understanding of your Purpose.

There are a number of ways of using this process. Some like to do the seven questions in one go... it takes about 90 minutes. Look at your watch... in an hour and a half you could know your Purpose. Cool, eh? Other people like to sip the process, doing one question a week for seven weeks. They dive deeply into the pool of contemplation and swim in their answers for a while. Both are good.

The process is quick because the questions are asked of your creative-intuitive mind, which has little or no blocks. It is a quick-and-easy route into your deepest self. You already have all the answers you need, your Purpose will feel familiar and true to you, like an old friend.

Two of the seven questions have multiple parts or stages to them. For example, the Desert Island Question and the Superhero Question each has three parts. Each question is written on one page while on the facing page are some "tips and tricks" to help you give your truest, most effective answer. Once you've answered these questions, you will be guided to write your Purpose statement.

The programme works best if you take it stage by stage and try not to skip or jump ahead. I suggest you read the book with a notepad and a pen handy so you are ready to answer these questions as you go through them. Some people like to keep a special notebook for their Purpose and insights. Many people I know go through the questions once a year, not because their answers fundamentally differ but because they give rise to other levels of insight. If you keep these answers in a special book or on your phone you can compare them more easily later.

Creativity and intuition

I have learned that I cannot live my Purpose when I am in survival mode.

Apparently the birth of language in us as a species happened when we learned how to create fire. Up until that point we were instinct-based, constantly on the alert for danger from any sabre-toothed thing that happened to be lurking in our cave-dwelling vicinity. All our instincts were honed to survival. We were fairly easy prey and we had to stick together to give weight in numbers when fearsome creatures came along... and who knew when they would swing by?

And then we created fire. Suddenly everything that might eat us was afraid of the dancing light. When we were around the fire we were safe for the first time. That safety and peace meant we could stop looking over our hairy shoulders and start to imagine. Imagination gave birth to new possibilities. There was then a need and desire to communicate those new possibilities – and language was born.

So, do we wait until we have moved beyond "survival" in our day-to-day lives – paid off the mortgage, secured our children's future, got the job that's going to set us up for life – to start living our Purpose?

The philosopher Andrew Cohen said that we as human beings live better today than any king, queen, emperor, empress, sultan or sultana in history. We have more access to choice, to warmth, light, heat, travel and so on.

If we can retain that fact in day-to-day life, perhaps we could perceive ourselves as living beyond survival. Think about it: if you can read this your survival is pretty much assured. You will pretty much always have a roof over your head, enough clothes, food, warmth and companionship to ensure a standard of living that exceeds that of 99 per cent of society in all of history.

I recently walked past a homeless person in London. As I was giving them some money for the magazine they were selling, their mobile phone went off. I said to her, "Hang on a sec' – you are homeless and asking me for money and yet you have a smartphone?" She looked at me as if I was insane... "Of course. How else am I going to keep in touch with people?" This person is on the "bottom rung" of society in financial terms and yet in her pocket she carries a space-age piece of technology.

It's worth us remembering when we put ourselves into survival mode that we still have infinite choices – so in a way, we're not really in survival mode. We always have the option of Purposeful living.

When you answer the seven questions, you should set aside some safe, warm, fireside time. The questions will ignite your imagination and a new, deeply familiar, possibility will reveal itself to you.

The imagination of our ancestors drove their evolution. It will be your imagination that drives yours. The fire they relied upon to give them safety is a warm, quiet place you can come home to. Give yourself to yourself. Nobody else can or will do that for you.

The "YES factor"

Lots of people say that it takes years to discover your Purpose and they are sceptical that it can be done in the time it takes to watch a film. They pose the question: "If it's that easy and quick, can I really trust that my Purpose statement is true for me?" The answer, of course, is YES – and there's a measure that we will put in place to ensure your conviction. I call it the "YES factor" and it works like this: at every stage of the process and phase of each question you will be asked the question "how much does your answer say 'YES' to you on a scale of one to ten". (This is going to happen a lot, so it's best to get used to it.) Put down the answer that feels authentic and spontaneous. We only action eights and above. Abandon any answer below an eight or use the "tips and tricks" section on the facing page to pop it up the scale.

An eight is an A in examination vernacular. If we can achieve a six or a seven we can most definitely achieve an eight. When people are eight-out-of-ten bought into something – an action, an outcome, an idea – they are prepared to take action around it. When they fall below an eight, they are not. Eight and above means a level of commitment, enthusiasm and engagement.

At every step of the way you will be giving answers to the questions that are eight, nine or ten out ten for you. That means you are bought in intellectually, emotionally and intuitively. That's commitment. Your final Purpose statement will be the culmination of a sequence of these eights, nines, tens so you can be certain that the answers you gave are a true and authentic representation of who you really are.

Here are a few examples to give you an idea of how the "YES factor" works:

1. Food

Someone says to you, "Fancy pizza for lunch?" You think, "Hmmm that's a six for me." A seven might be... a sandwich. An eight might be... "That new cafe down the road looks good." A nine: "Actually, I would love an amazing salad followed by the world's greatest coffee." A ten... you get the idea. Once we start putting our answers on the scale it's easy to pop them up.

2. Email

Do you ever receive those loooong, wordy paragraph emails? Are they the first to be read or the last to be read? How often, when we are writing an email, do we ask ourselves the question: "How much does this say what I want it to say in content and tone on a scale of one to ten?" If we're honest with ourselves, we find that we send out quite a few mails which are below an eight. If we spend another minute popping that email up so it's an eight, nine or ten, lots of things change. Some people say that their emails become shorter and more succinct. Others say that they stop cc'ing lots of other people into the email, or they give examples, or they improve the subject line and so on. Invariably, though, their communication improves and thus so does the result.

3. Bigger things

Years ago I remember running a series of seminars for a top multi-national. It was a great programme – helping people live by their values and make those values part of their business and personal decision-making. Throughout the course we had been encouraging participants to apply the "YES factor" to all their thoughts, actions and decisions. It was very successful. A week or so after the end of the programme we were sitting in a room with the head of learning and development, who said: "Great job. Fabulous course. That was definitely a ten for me." I remember shrivelling inwardly as I realized that the course was a seven for me. It was great fun, highly effective and delivered everything the client wanted and more, but for me it was a seven. That weekend, all my foundations shook. I knew that I had gone as far as I could go with that particular way of working and that I could not stand in front of groups and say "only action eights and above" when I myself was on a seven. The question then became: "What's eight, nine or ten for you, Rich?"

I spent the weekend contemplating, discussing and listening. By Sunday night I had realized that I wanted to go back to theatre. It was a nine or ten out of ten for me. I couldn't see how that would work business-wise, but it was above a seven and that was what I was going to do. "Let the chips fall where they may."

On the Tuesday morning after, I received an email out of the blue from a local authority asking if I would be interested in pitching for a piece of work training 10,000 people using interactive theatre. "Er… yes," I typed back. We went on to deliver the project. It was definitely a nine or ten for me. We won awards for it, launched a movement of positivity and possibility in a part of the UK that had experienced economic depression for two generations. We changed our lives and that of thousands of others.

Eight, nine or ten out of ten is the only choice. Everything else is settling for a compromise and choosing to be unsatisfied.

That process has to be applied in the chapter that follows: The Seven Questions. All you have to do is answer the questions honestly and openly, making sure that each answer you give says "YES" to you on a core level – eight, nine or ten out of ten. If it's an eight, nine or ten keep it. If it's not, change it.

2

The Seven Questions

Answering the Seven Questions

B efore you launch into the seven questions there are a number of things you should consider.

1. All at once?

Often people like to sit down and answer all the questions in one sitting. Answering the questions all at once brings a momentum to our discovery and facilitates the process. As I have said, some people prefer to answer one question over a set period of time, such as a week or a month, and really chew on the contemplations. Both ways work. This is, after all, a guided contemplation. How you choose to engage with it is up to you. My suggestion, though, is that once you start you see it through to the end. When the "to do" list starts piling up, the phone is buzzing and a tempest of emails is calling for your attention there is a temptation to say "this is not a priority, I'll wait till I have more time". You won't. That's myth. If your Purpose is not a priority in your life, neither is your happiness and fulfilment. If you cannot find 90 minutes to find out what is your richest relationship to life then you absolutely need to do this. Time is the most important commodity that you possess. Put it toward the things that are the most life-enhancing and nourishing.

2. One at a time

This process speaks to your creative-intuitive mind, enabling you to find your most truthful responses effortlessly, regardless of how much your logical mind likes to block them. The questions are very specific and are designed to be answered in a particular order. Don't read ahead; it's counterproductive. You only get once chance to make a first impression. If you look ahead, and then decide to go back and answer the questions, you will colour your answers and deprive yourself of the freshness that spontaneity brings. Please read one question at a time and observe the special conditions of each. Some questions require you to answer in less than ten words, others ask you for seven suggestions. Some take a single premise and reimagine them in several contexts. The questions are designed to help you get to clarity and to engage the richest part of your consciousness... and they work. Thousands of people have been through this process. They either arrive at an understanding that brings new light and clarity on the direction of their lives, or their answers serve as a deep reassurance about the choices they have taken. All you have to do is be completely honest in your answers, as if nobody else will ever see what you have written. You cannot get the answers wrong.

3. Trust your answers

The questions are asked in scenarios which plough the imagination as a path to self-reflection and insight. The logical mind puts up obstacles which obstruct us in the discovery of our greatest potential. It operates mostly in the status quo, comparing ourselves to other people and fitting in. The problem with that is that most people are living unconsciously, with no knowledge of their Purpose or of what drives them truly. If we are constantly trying to fit ourselves to the status quo we are cutting and pasting other people's dysfunctions onto our future. Or as Robin Williams once said: "That's like going hunting with Ray Charles." If I ask someone, "What's your Purpose?", most people cannot answer the question. It does not mean they do not know, only that the question is not helpful. It is too vast; there are too many implications. Therefore we need to break it down a bit, looking at the component parts of Purpose and leading you there through the garden of the unconscious mind rather than the traffic jam of the logical one. We approach the questions through the fertile realms of the imagination, the golden bridge uniting the conscious and the subconscious. Most people are unfamiliar with the workings of their subconscious. That's OK. The questions ask you to give your intuitive response and then "pop" them up the "YES factor" scale to an eight, nine or ten out of ten. You have to trust what comes to you through your imagination and intuition. Listen to the first response that comes to you, even if it is accompanied by a little nagging voice telling you that it's not what you'd normally consider doing. As Nelson Mandela famously quoted Marianne Williamson: "Our deepest fear is not that we are inadequate. Our deepest fear is that we are powerful beyond measure. It is our light, not our darkness that most frightens us."

4. Use the "tips and tricks"

On the page facing the question are "tips and tricks" to help you articulate your answers clearly and Purposefully. These will help you to move your answers up the "YES factor" scale, making sure that you get to an eight, nine or ten and giving the best to yourself.

I recommend using the "tips and tricks" after putting down your initial response and see if they change or enhance what you have done. Sometimes the tips are alternative ways of asking the same question, sometimes the phrasing of the question is reshaped to help you come to an intuitive response.

5. No examples

I never give examples of what others say or write in response to the questions, with one exception (The Tombstone Question). When we hear examples something inside us says, "Ah OK, I have to write something like that." You don't. Write what is true for you. That is the only truth there is in this instance and the only one you are ultimately interested in. We are all unique and our Purpose reflects this. Once we have completed the questioning process we will explore your answers. For the moment, though, we must have the courage to see the best in ourselves, whether or not that coincides with any one else's point of view.

6. Uphold honesty and integrity

Be honest, it will save a lot of time and effort. Honesty is the cornerstone of integrity and the gateway to truth. Many people think that being honest is "owning up to their bad points". At a Purpose workshop for a top pharmaceutical company – with 250 high achievers in the same room – people were asked to share some of their answers following the seven questions. The room went very quiet. I then asked them if they could tell me what about them wasn't "good enough". Lots of comments and lots of hands went up. I said to them, "Why is it that you are delighted to talk about all the things you consider to be weak or poor about yourself but when I ask you to share your best or the most beautiful part of yourself tumbleweeds blow across the room?" My experience is that people are far more loving, kind and giving than they give themselves credit for. Allow your honesty to shine your brightness and dissolve your obstacles. It will bring you to a greater truth in your answers and in your life.

7. Discover the "diamond" of Purpose

Some people get a bit jittery just before they start answering the questions, asking things like: "Do I have to commit to this Purpose for the rest of my life?" "Does this mean I can't change my mind later?" "This is a bit like deciding to marry someone I haven't yet met. How do I know that I am making the right choice for me?" These are all good questions, but they are not going to help. Essentially each question is designed to assist you to find the most meaningful answers from within. They come from you, for you. So if you don't like the answers enough to commit to them, choose ones that you can commit to. It's a bit like being given some money and told to go shopping for things that you absolutely love; would you say, "But if I find something I absolutely adore, do I have to have it?" The answer, of course, is no – but if you absolutely *adore* it, why wouldn't you want it?

Our Purpose is like the spine in our bodies. It is within us all the time in every action we perform and everywhere we go. Yet, as mentioned earlier, if we sit still and try to "feel" our spine, we can't do it. It doesn't mean that our spine isn't there, only that our awareness is not acute enough to feel it. The "diamond" of Purpose resides deep within us, locked there like our spine, and yet for some reason we may never have felt it or identified it. This process is about uncovering the first facet of that diamond. The Purpose statement you will write at the end of the seven questions will name that first facet. Once you have discovered this facet you will start to see others. All these facets have a slightly different hue and yet they are all part of the same gem.

For the time being, find a quiet place, sharpen the pencil, have a notebook in front of you and get your mind and body into that Sunday-afternoon-squashy-armchair-comfortable-smell-of-hot-buttered-toast space and settle into some gentle humming contemplation.

Here goes...

1. The Desert Island Question

PART 1

You and a number of others, enough to make up a small community, are stranded on a desert island. It is an eight-, nine- or ten-out-of-ten desert island, whatever that means to you. There is plenty of food, water and shelter, so survival is not a problem. The winds and tides dictate that you will have to stay here for a good amount of time, and the geography of the island is such that you cannot live on your own.

Write a few lines describing your eight-, nine- or ten-out-of-ten desert island and then answer the following two questions:

1. How do you choose to actively contribute to this society?

2. How do you choose to nourish yourself in this environment?

Tips and Tricks

i. It really helps to imagine or write a paragraph describing your eight-, nine- or ten-out-of-ten island. It makes your choices clearer and easier to access.

ii. Please answer the questions purely, without interpretation. Interpretation thinks things like: "He probably means, what would I be likely to do?" The question is absolute. In the circumstances of the scenario, *how do you choose to actively contribute* to this society?

iii. List a maximum of six answers. When you feel like your answer is complete, "YES factor" it. That is, look at each suggestion and ask: How much does this say "YES" to me out of ten? Make sure that your answers say "YES" to you eight, nine or ten out of ten. If they don't, ask yourself what you could do to actively contribute that would say "YES" to you at an eight, nine or ten out of ten? Alternatively, you could put the question like this. If I were to actively contribute in a way that says "YES" to me nine out of ten I would probably do something like...

Whatever comes to you in that moment is likely to be your nine-out-of-ten suggestion. Trust your intuition.

iv. "How do you choose to nourish yourself?" This is asking what you choose to do just for you. This could mean activities with other people or you could be on your own, but the activities don't have to contribute to anyone else apart from you. What would you do to generate a quality of life that says "YES" to you eight, nine or ten out of ten?

v. Choose your top one, two or three answers, depending on how many you have written down, and get ready to move on. We are not looking to draw any conclusions at this stage, only to answer the questions.

vi. Finally, if there was such a thing as a ten-out-of-ten response to a question, it would be something like...

Write down your answers.

The Desert Island Question

PART 2

So… you build a raft to leave the first desert island (see page 30) and the winds and tides eventually land you on the shores of a second island. If the first island was an eight-, nine- or ten-out-of-ten island for you on your "YES factor" scale, this island is a five, six or seven out of ten, whatever that means to you. There is plenty of food, water and shelter for you, so survival is not an issue. You have to stay on this island for a good amount of time until conditions change and the geography of the island dictates that you have to live in the community there.

Write a few lines describing your five-, six- or seven-out-of-ten desert island and then answer the following questions:

1. How do you choose to actively contribute to this society?

2. How do you choose to nourish yourself in this environment?

Tips and Tricks

i. Imagine or write a paragraph describing your five-, six- or seven-out-of-ten island. What are the differences between this island and your first one? What makes it more of a five-, six- or seven-out-of-ten island than an eight-, nine- or ten-out-of-ten island?

ii. As before, "YES factor" your answers. They must score eight, nine or ten out of ten. This can be measured both in terms of enjoyment and appropriateness – that is, how appropriate does this answer feel out of ten?

iii. Your answers may be the same as or different to those for the previous island.

iv. If any of your answers are seven or below try the following questions to help you "pop" them up the scale:

    a. What sort of things would you be doing to actively contribute and nourish yourself if you were on an eight-out-of-ten island or on a nine-out-of-ten island?

    b. A nine-out-of-ten answer feels/looks/would probably be something like...

    c. If you could choose to do something with absolute ten-out-of-ten certainty, what would that be?

v. Choose your top one, two or three answers depending on how many you have written down, and get ready to move on.

The Desert Island Question

PART 3

The day comes when you leave this island. You take your raft and head out to sea back toward the first island or beyond. The winds and tides have another plan, however, and you are washed up on the shores of a third desert island. If the last island was a five, six, or seven out of ten, this one is definitely a two, three or four out of ten, whatever that means to you. There is still plenty of food, water and shelter for you, so survival is not an issue. You have to stay on this island for a good amount of time and the geography of the island dictates that you have to live in the community there.

1.How do you choose to actively contribute to this society?

2.How do you choose to nourish yourself in this environment?

Tips and Tricks

i. Imagine or write a paragraph describing your two-, three- or four-out-of-ten desert island. What is it like? What circumstances or factors make this island different from the ones before?

ii. Whatever restrictions are placed on you by this situation and/or environment, you are still required to make choices which are an eight, nine or ten on your "YES factor" scale, both in terms of appropriateness and satisfaction.

iii. Your answers may be the same as or different to those for the previous island.

iv. Push yourself. Come up with at least three nine-out-of-ten suggestions. What would you have to give in this environment? How could you give it?

v. Find failsafe ways to nourish yourself.

vi. If you were eight , nine- or ten-out-of-ten successful in putting your plans into action, how would life be for you here? "YES factor" your answers.

vii. If it were possible to have ten-out-of-ten answers they would be things like...

Your answers to this question give you a strategy to live in the ten zone even if the outside world does not support this.

2. The Tombstone Question

If there was one word that describes how you would most like to be remembered, to be etched onto your tombstone for evermore, what would that word to be?

Before you answer this question have a look at the "tips and tricks". It will help...

Tips and Tricks

i. The question is very specific. It does not say "How am I likely to be remembered" or "How do I think people would describe me?" The only question to answer is: *How would you most like to be remembered?* It's a key distinction.

ii. Sometimes it can be hard to answer a question like this straight out. So here is a process to make things simpler, more enjoyable and more complete. I call it "semantic blending". Choose seven words that describe how you would like to be remembered and then "YES factor" them. For example, honourable, kind, noble, compassionate, giving, loving and generous.

iii. If there is one word that stands out as being "the One" choose that. It may be that you can't pick one out; in which case, here's a way to find that word. Look at your list and see which words naturally go together. It is likely that among your seven words there are some with a similar meaning – like different facets of the same diamond. From the examples above, I would instinctively group together:

honourable + noble

compassionate + loving + kind

giving + generous

This makes three separate groups. Now choose one word to represent each of those groups so that you end up with only three words:

For example, honourable + noble = noble (for me nobility of character includes honour). However, I could also put "honest" down because this speaks to me in a similar way. It's a personal choice.

Compassionate + loving = loving, because for me "loving" necessarily includes compassion, especially in its eight-, nine- or ten-out-of-ten form. For you, of course, it may be different – there's no right or wrong, just eight, nine or ten.

Kind + giving + generous = kind

The next step is to try to merge your three words to get one that says "YES" to you nine or ten out of ten. See what the seven different qualities suggest to you. Sometimes they are obvious, sometimes surprising and delightful. This is a wonderful and elegant exercise and well worth remembering for other situations. It moves you beyond words into deeper meaning and that, of course, is the landscape of Purpose.

Watch out

Sometimes people get cold feet about how beautiful and moving their words are. They say to themselves, "What would people think if I described myself like that; I'll have to tone it down a bit." It's OK; you don't have to show this to anyone, it's just for you. Remember this is how you would most like to be remembered. Someone else, ultimately, would be writing this on your tombstone, not you. The only thing that matters is your authentic answer to this question. Write down the word that is true for you in spite of any cynicism or internal criticism you may encounter... leave that outside the door. All cynics claim that they are realists. They are not, though... cynicism is not truth.

So... noble + kind might = ?...true.

True + loving might = ?... true or truthful

I did this exercise once and the three words I was working on blending were: knightly, generous and kind. I held the quality of each word, felt into them and blended them as I would a sauce and the word "shepherd" emerged in the steam of my concoction. It was beautiful and deeply resonant for me. It spoke to me more than any of the previous words could have done and yet it would never have been on my original list of seven. Sometimes other words hold a stronger meaning for us.

We're dancing with the conscious and unconscious minds. Trust what says "YES" to you most. Keep to one word if possible and use one that is in daily language as opposed to making it up. It will embolden you later.

When you have your word ask yourself how happy you would be if it were etched onto your tombstone after your death, and if your answer is nine or ten out of ten this question is complete.

You can test the word out for yourself by running it through your head – "Here lies [my name], 'True'. Rest In Peace."

Write down your final word under a little RIP in a tombstone sketch.

Some people wonder if they are being arrogant attributing such wonderful qualities to themselves. Arrogance is not self-assurance, it is a compensation for a feeling of inadequacy. This process is about

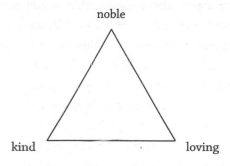

determining what your values and aspirations are. By choosing a word you are not saying that this is the way you are all of the time, or even most of the time, you are simply saying that this word stands for something which is nine- or ten-out-of-ten important to you and you would love this word to be a constant theme in your life.

Make sure you have one word that speaks to you at an eight, nine or ten out of ten before moving on to answer the next question.

3. The *Book of Life* Question

Imagine there is a *Book of Life*. Everyone has a paragraph in the book consisting of three sentences. The entry describes what this person *gave* in their lifetime. What would you like your entry to say?

Tips and Tricks

i. Fulfilment comes from what we give more than from what we get. There are as few deeply fulfilled wealthy people as there are poor people. This entry is written from the perspective of someone at the culmination of a life well lived.

ii. Restricting your answer to less than 15 words will help you get to clarity. Clarity is a key to unlocking self-confidence and self-knowledge.

iii. "YES factor" yourself on how clean and well defined your entry is. Be as specific as you can. Generalization will not get you where you want to go.

iv. When you have completed your entry, look to see if you are saying essentially the same thing in two or more of the sentences. If so, how would the sentences read were you to combine them? If you do that, you will have space for a new, third sentence. What would that be? What would be the icing on the cake?

v. If you have written your sentences in less than 15 words, how few words can you use to write your entry with the same or greater impact? Try using five words – it will get you to the essence of what you want to give.

vi. Hard to answer? Try this:

Imagine it is at least 100 years into the future. You are a disembodied spirit hanging around the pearly gates of Heaven and you see the Archangel Gabriel talking to the bookkeeper and a number of other saints. You glance over their shoulder and, lo and behold, your name is at the top of the page, with three sentences underneath describing what you gave.

They read…

    1.

    2.

    3.

4. The Song-Slogan Question

Imagine for a moment that there were another part of you, a "light-shadow" if you like, that went with you everywhere. It can speak, sing, move and dance but is almost completely invisible and inaudible to others. Almost but not completely. Now, imagine that it were to sing out a song-slogan to the world at the top of its voice, 24 hours a day, seven days a week, every week of the year.

What would you like your song-slogan to be?

Tips and Tricks

i. A song-slogan is a short message or phrase that means something to you. It could be from a song you already know, if that says "YES" to you at an eight, nine or ten out of ten, or you can make one up.

   If you are going to hear it somewhere in your being 24 hours per day, seven days a week, you may as well make it a nine- or ten-out-of-ten slogan.

ii. If you're struggling with this one, imagine you love life, are passionate about the world in a sunshiny way and that you have to sing a song-slogan (a maximum of five words) expressing your state or giving a simple message to be sung out to the world – you would sing something like...

How much does your answer say "YES" to you out of ten?

5. The World-Microphone Question

Imagine that there is a "world-microphone", a device that broadcasts on every piece of media on the planet simultaneously – every television and radio station, cinema screen, website, newspaper, magazine, book, newsletter... everything, all at the same time.

In a short while, you will have sole use of the world-microphone for 15 minutes. How do you use your time? What is your message? Write a sentence, a paragraph or a page describing what you would say. Your answer must say "YES" to you on a core level nine or ten out of ten.

Tips and Tricks

i. Make the situation real for yourself. If you really had access to such a tool, what is the best use you could make of it? And what is your core message?

ii. What does your answer tell you is so important to you that you would use your 15 minutes of fame in this way?

If you can write a nine-out-of-ten answer, what is a ten?

iii. An alternative question for those who imagine themselves afraid of public speaking: If somehow you could whisper a message into the ear of every person on the planet while they slept, what would it be?

6. The Superhero Question

PART 1

If you were a superhero, what seven powers would you most like to have?

1.
2.
3.
4.
5.
6.
7.

What would your superhero name be?

Tips and Tricks

i. You can have established superhero powers, such as being able to fly or breathe underwater, and new ones you make up for yourself. There is no limit to what you can have. You decide.

ii. Try to invent at least three of your powers. It will stretch you and you will get more out of the contemplation. "YES factor" each answer. Only put down ones which truly say "YES" to you eight, nine or ten out of ten.

iii. Make sure you complete this section, putting down all seven powers.

iv. Please do not turn over the page until you have completed this section.

The Superhero Question

PART 2

This question does not make sense. Please answer it anyway. If, in two weeks' time, you wake up in the morning and discover you have one of the seven powers you wrote down, which one is it *most likely* to be?

Tips and Tricks

i. I know. It doesn't make any sense – which one is it most likely to be?
Not, which one would I most like it to be? That's a different question
and nothing to do with this one. The question is, which one is it most
likely to be? Whether that makes sense or not, please answer it. We
will find out why later.

The Superhero Question

PART 3

In two weeks' time you wake up in the morning and discover that you have this one power.

1. Realistically, what do you do with it?

2. What's the best you could do with it?

Tips and Tricks

i. Your answers must say "YES" nine or ten out of ten. No surprises there.

Imagine, really, waking up in the morning and having this power or ability. How do you choose to use it for the greater good? If it's not for the greater good, are you really a superhero?

ii. If you have an eight-out-of-ten answer, a nine might be more like...

iii. What's the best use you can imagine for this power? What could give you the most satisfaction and fulfilment when it is put into action? How would life be if this were true and you really followed through? What would your life in the modern world be like?

iv. This may all seem like fantasy time, but it will all make sense later.

7. What is the Purpose I Serve?

You're nearly there now. Well played.

Looking over and digesting all that you have written and considered, complete the following sentence using ten words or less, in a way which says "YES" to you at a nine or ten out of ten.

I serve the Purpose of...

Tips and Tricks

i. Please keep the phrasing of the sentence. Sometimes people are tempted to change it to "My Purpose is..." This is less powerful and less active. Your Purpose must, necessarily, be larger than you – that is, something you serve, and act upon. "I serve the Purpose of" implies both.

ii. Make it a "YES factor" of nine out of ten... you know the drill.

iii. Make it clean, solid and complete. If what you have written is true for you, it will feel powerful and have an expansive quality in that the more you think about it the more implications it has.

iv. If you can complete the sentence in less than five words, what would it be? Write the longer version first and then refine it down. "YES factor" your short version. Does it feel more complete and powerful than the original?

v. Imagine living true to this Purpose every day of your life. How fulfilled would you feel? How might your life be different in five years' time?

vi. Your Purpose statement does not have to mean anything to anyone else. It is for you and you alone. The true fulfilment comes from living it, not telling it.

vii. Is it likely to be meaningful to you in six months' time? How about in a year? Ten years?

viii. What Purpose can you truly serve ten out of ten?

ix. If you feel a sense of achievement, of warmth and excitement, or as though the sun is shining inside – well done, you've found your Purpose in life. Celebrate. You rock!

Exploring your Answers –
Question by Question

Your Purpose is not to get rich, your Purpose is to BE rich. To enrich yourself and your experience of the present moment. That is done by investing ourselves in all that we are and all that we do. Both feet in.

You have now named your Purpose, the first facet of your "diamond". When you look at your Purpose statement and read the sentence through to yourself, it should feel true to who you are – as if it were something you always knew but had never named. You have named the first facet of your "diamond" but much more to the point is the fact that you have been listening. In every part of every question you have asked yourself, "How much does this say 'YES' to me out of ten?" You now know what being in the two, three or four zone is like... how the five, six or seven zone feels and, of course, the eight, nine or ten zone. And nobody had to teach you how to do it. You were just asked to make it a rule of engagement, like brushing your teeth, and you did it. Simply put, whenever you need to make a decision about anything, from what you want for lunch to which country you want to live in, "YES factor" it. When you're above an eight, you're in the Purpose zone. Your experiences will be in accordance with that.

The more you seek out the eights, nines or tens the more you will become attuned to those types of experiences and the less appetite you will have for the fives, sixes or sevens. It's an upgrade and a beautiful one. It is not without its side effects too. As Muhammad Ali recounted John Lennon saying to him when they met at a party: "The more real you get, the more unreal all this is going to seem." Meaning all the press, hangers on and accoutrements of celebrity...

Within that Purpose zone there's another quality too, a sense that it was waiting to be discovered, a "meant to be-ness".

I want you to live your Purpose in life. It's best for you, it's best for me and it's best for the planet. Everybody wins. More than that – or at least equal with that – is my desire to put you in touch with your inner knowing. I have learned enough as a teacher, trainer and facilitator to know that the greatest, wisest and most robust knowledge comes from within. My mission is to get you started – and the questions give you a way of listening to that deeply personal source of power and authenticity. They are a way of engaging with the day. You know how to listen for the eight, nine or ten and to mine that part of your consciousness.

The following section, based upon the seven questions, is designed to broaden and deepen your experience of your Purpose and to engage with your subconscious as a playmate so that the adventure of conscious unfolding begins and gathers momentum. Finding and naming your Purpose is not the same as living it. A compass bearing is not the journey, it is just the starting point for the adventure. Your subconscious is truly remarkable. There is a whole world of discovery in each answer, so initially we will look more deeply at your answers to the questions. We'll then address making the adventure happen for each question through a series of experiments and principles, which will help to explore and play with your Purpose every day in every part of your life.

1. The Desert Island Question

The magician Derren Brown did an extraordinary trick. He asked two advertising creatives to join him for an experiment. He sent a taxi, which then delivered them via a pre-arranged route to the studio. When he met the two men he gave them a very open brief to come up with an advertising slogan for a taxidermist. When they eventually came up with their image and slogan he revealed the one that he had drawn a week or so before they came into the studio. The two images and even the slogans were almost exactly the same. Free will wasn't really free will. He showed how he had planted subliminal suggestions in the two unsuspecting ad men during their taxi ride by using shop windows, street signs and the windows of parked cars. The "taxi" in taxidermist had reminded them of their ride and then in their "free" association, their subconscious minds had locked onto the iconic images he had placed along the way.

How many of our free choices in life are really free? Do we choose our romantic partners because they remind us of our parents? Do we make career choices because of the negative or positive influences of teachers or family? Do we choose our clothes because of the film heroes with whom we identify?

I am not suggesting that any of these choices are wrong for us in any way. They may be perfect. However, isn't it worth taking a moment and giving ourselves the opportunity to strip away our influences as much as possible and see what choices we would make then? Could that reveal our innate desires, the ones which are perfectly suited to our unique set of talents as opposed to the school curriculum?

A desert island is a place where we can be truly free – from social pressures, distractions of the modern world and even responsibilities. Our needs are minimal and because having food, water and shelter is a given, we are free to make the choices which say "YES" to us most.

Whatever you chose, then, is what you would choose from a place of freedom… The good news is, you are free. So, if you simply start to action those choices in an intelligent way, you will be living your eight, nine or ten life.

Looking back over your answers:

What do you notice about your responses to the first part of the question in each of the three scenarios – how do you choose to actively contribute to that environment?

Are there any similarities and consistent themes that show up? Are they significantly different or the same? What do your answers tell you?

How about your choices about nourishing yourself?

If we are giving according to our gifts in harmony with the whole and at the same time nourishing ourselves, we can make sure that we are in a state of expansion not sacrifice – the best of ourselves for the highest good of the whole. That, after all, is our Purpose.

In knowing how, from a place of freedom, we would choose to nourish ourselves, we get to understand what warms our heart and is integral to our being. Engaging in these activities helps us in every area of our life. It is likely that we are already doing these things; however, many of us get caught up in a hailstorm of distractions, buried beneath in-trays of "must dos", and we forget to give to ourselves, which doesn't help us to give our best. If we are giving to others eight, nine or ten out of ten and giving to ourselves two, three or four out of ten we will burn out pretty quickly. We have to put fuel in our car to give others a lift home.

What did you choose to do to nourish yourself throughout the spectrum of islands?

Are you doing these things now?

If not, your free choice has shown you this is how you like to generate your well-being. To nourish yourself you now have a strategy if you choose it.

Which environment speaks loudest to you of your current situation in life?

In the island scenarios, what helpful ways of dealing with these situations did you identify that you could apply now?

What constitutes a two, three or four and a five, six or seven environment? Are there any similarities?

Your answers to these questions show you how you would find the greatest happiness for yourself and give the best you have to offer no matter how inhospitable the outside world is.

If you answered the questions with a "YES factor" of eight, nine or ten, it proves that your imagination can furnish you with enlightened choices in all situations. It's like having a universal "get out of jail free" card.

If you can generate eight, nine or ten experiences in a two , three or four environment, you are free.

Experiments

What would you say are your current two, three or four environments or situations?

What are your current five, six or seven environments or situations?

How can you live eight, nine or ten experiences even in these environments?

Do you need to nourish yourself differently or more? Do you want to contribute in a different way?

What's your eight, nine or ten right now and how can you get one point closer to it?

2. The Tombstone Question

Who, on their deathbed, ever said that they wished they'd spent more time in the office or surrounded by bank statements?

How much of our lives is spent focused on "getting"? On accomplishing something? As if the Purpose of life was to accumulate things. People get a "status" hit from cars, from their level in the hierarchy at work, the labels on their clothes, you name it. Status by its very nature says: "I'm better than you because...." It doesn't really matter what it's focused around, the whole premise is flawed. Better than, worse than – it's irrelevant. The accumulation of things, whether as a false pursuit or as a route to status, rarely gets us where we want to go. The only thing that matters in life is our experience of it. Our experience. It's the only thing that's real and... it's within us. Our perspective determines our reality.

The Tombstone Question is a very important one. It asks us to decide which values and qualities mean the most to us. When we know what our true values are we have a direct route into our inner being. We know how we want to live, not according to the cut-out images of a disposable society but in sync with what's real. It's the perspective that takes us to the only freedom there is.

The words you put down to get to your tombstone words describe your values. How could they not? I have never heard anyone when asked for a word that they would like to be etched on their tombstone to describe themselves who has answered "arrogant", "overbearing", "controlling", "slim", "timid", "flashy", "powerful" or even "successful". Yet these words and others like them can describe our behaviour day in and day out. A new-born baby has no idea that it can control its limbs. After a while of seeing a little fist or foot shoot past its head it starts to make the link that somehow it is connected to this phenomena. After a while it relates its thoughts with these seemingly random movements and the process of mastering physical movement begins.

The same is true for us. We live a whole spectrum of experiences. We can be loving, kind, compassionate, funny, enchanting, cheeky, sexy, sedate, arrogant, grumpy, mean, self-obsessed and pretty much any adjective you can think of. It can seem as if these feelings are happening to us, like the baby's hand shooting past its face. However, we only experience these feelings as a result of our inner perspective. If we could connect to the values which drive our healthiest and truest perspective on life perhaps we would have more experiences which reflect the best of ourselves and thus the best of life.

So now you have a list. You know what your values are. You were free to put down anything you wanted. You might have written "flamboyant" or "discreet" – both are equally worthy. It was your eight, nine or ten choice. If you gave yourself to the process, these words mean something to you. Your final tombstone word came from a process of inclusion not exclusion. We have built and embedded meaning in the final word so that it speaks of all those words that went into it... like marinating a piece of fish before cooking it.

Then the question becomes... how do we live these words more? How can they become our dominant experience of ourselves? How can we cultivate them and – if we want a boost for that cultivation – how do we play with them?

Experiments

If you were to know how much you are living this value or quality in your life right now on a scale of one to ten, you would probably say... If it is below ten and you were going to live it one point up on the scale, name three things you would do differently... If you were going to pop up another point...

Take the last month of your life and write it as a chapter in a story. Now rewrite it as if you had lived your tombstone word at an eight, nine or ten out of ten.

Name a character from a film or book who is a great example of this value? If you watch the film or read the book, what do you learn about that value or quality?

Experiment with dressing as this quality. What would that change? How does it feel? What does it encourage you to do or feel? Does it feel more you or less you? What aspect of you is that quality and how much are you living it in your life currently?

All seven words you chose and your final choice represent your values; the more you live them, the more Value-able you are.

3. The *Book of Life* Question

"Days are like scrolls. Write on them what you want remembered."
The Talmud

Giving and receiving are one. Our in-breath and out-breath are not separate things, they are one... breathing. You cannot do one without the other. If all we did was breathe in, we would suffocate as surely as if all we did was breathe out. Giving without receiving is sacrifice, which by definition means doing something for others at the expense of yourself. Giving without expectation of receiving has long been lauded as an admirable quality. The one who suffers for the sake of the whole is one of the definitions of heroes in popular culture. That's a bit like applauding people who breathe out until they die or experience brain damage, instead of completing the gesture by breathing in again afterwards. Giving and receiving are part of the same cycle, neither more worthy than the other. Is the back of your hand more worthy than the palm? Ridiculous isn't it?

There is an exercise I do with people called the Behaviour Map, where I ask people to take a skill, such as communication or creativity, and determine what they are like when they are living that skill two, three or four out of ten and then eight, nine or ten out of ten. For 25 years the results of this exercise have been consistent. When people identify how they think and behave when they are communicating two, three or four out of ten they describe an experience that is more cut off from others. When they describe their eight, nine or ten experience it always involves greater connection with other people, more openness, curiosity, generosity and willingness to explore.

People in peak state seem always to be in a mindset of giving and contributing. People who focus solely on themselves rarely live on an eight or above. Contribution and fulfilment are part and parcel of the same thing. By and large, *getting* separates whereas *giving* connects.

The *Book of Life* Question takes this perspective and wonders what three things you would like to have given by the time you shuffle off this mortal coil. Clarity breeds confidence and confidence leads to action.

If you ask someone what they want to achieve in life, they give you a big list. Some things are heartfelt; some are "expected", the natural trajectories of their current actions. That's not to say that these answers are not the ones that will lead to that person's fulfilment, it's that the nature of the question gives a focus and clarity. Limiting our possibilities to three sentences focuses our mind and prioritizes our choices. Phrasing the question as though we have lived our life and moved on takes the pressure off "achieving" and gives us perspective. When we have trekked up a mountain, pack on back, panting with the strain and get to the top we look back on the path we have taken and it brings our efforts into perspective. The same is true here. The "what if" releases a clarity we often can't get looking forward.

What do you get from this question? More to the point, what are you going to do with your answers?

Bronnie Ware, a palliative-care nurse, wrote a book called *The Top Five Regrets of the Dying*. The five regrets she identified were:

1. I wish I'd had the courage to live a life true to myself, not the life others expected of me.
2. I wish I hadn't worked so hard.
3. I wish I'd had the courage to express my feelings.
4. I wish I had stayed in touch with my friends.
5. I wish I had let myself be happier.

Courage to be oneself + a balance of work and life + relationships. That's it. That's what we want by and large.

You have three gorgeous sentences in your *Book of Life* answer.
You know now what you want.
Don't die without going for it.

Experiments

If you were to live one year in perfect health and you knew you would die at the end... what would you do in that time?

What if you had five years? How would you spend them?

Ten years? Write down your answers.

What, of all the things you have written down, will you action now?

4. The Song-Slogan Question

Although life makes sense, it doesn't necessarily to the mind. We place too much stock in the wisdom and effectiveness of our conscious minds and not enough in our unconscious abilities. Remember the 80:20 iceberg model? If we are going to create a path for our life that encompasses the whole of us – our fulfilment – we have to address the whole being. We have to start accessing our unconscious, deciphering it and respecting its unique language and style. How can we possibly explore our potential if we only plug away at 20 per cent of our capacity? That's like driving a car in first gear and wondering why we don't hit top speed.

We sing when we're happy. We sing to mark events, birthdays, national anthems and so on. We seek out certain types of music when we're sad, angry or contemplative. The music of the time is a direct reflection of society. During the 60s you could find The Beatles, Pink Floyd and Frank Sinatra side by side in the top ten of the music charts... mixed generations and world views squashed together. The birth of punk rock was an eruption of anger against the establishment.

Just as songs and music do in society, they reveal many layers in ourselves, and they do not have to make sense. A song can say "imagine all the people living life in Peace" or "wop-bop-alubop-a-wop-bam-boom" – both express perfectly what the writer felt when writing. And they express more than the words themselves, conveying a feeling, a vibe and an emotion.

There's an exercise I often do with groups, called the Chairs Game. Chairs are laid out randomly, facing different directions in a room. Everyone sits in a chair ("the sitters") with the exception of one person who will become "the walker". At the centre of the room is an empty chair. The walker's objective is to make their way to any empty chair and sit down; however, they are only allowed to walk at a slow pace. Everyone else's objective is to block the walker from sitting in an empty chair. They can move as fast as they like, but the moment they start to leave their chair they must completely vacate their position, regardless of whether or not it's the right thing to do. It's an hysterical game... an orchestra of panic. In theory the sitters should be able to block the walker for as long as they choose, but they rarely make it beyond five or ten seconds. As the sitters try again and again they work out different strategies for blocking the walker... the one who is furthest away moves, calls out a person's name to move, rotate from one chair to another, and so on. Each strategy is more complex than the next and each equally redundant. Eventually I show the group how to block the walker. There are two rules they need to obey:

1. The sitters need to move about 25 per cent faster than the walker. Just a bit faster.
2. The moment a sitter has decided to leave their chair, they must honour that movement and leave completely, even if it's the wrong thing to do.

Something amazing happens then – a kind of dance with freeform choreography. Just moving a little faster than the walker stops all the panic in the room. It increases people's awareness for the whole and settles them into a rhythm. Choosing to leave their seat the moment they feel the impulse means that they no longer have to think through all the possibilities and ramifications of their decision. When they leave their seat, as long as the others are moving about 25 per cent faster than the walker, they are covered. It doesn't matter if they make a mistake, someone has got their back. The solution to the exercise is not thinking, it's rhythm… a groove if you will. The same is true in a song-slogan. Even thinking about a song-slogan means that our imagination and therefore our subconscious engages with a rhythm… the groove of our Purpose. For some people it is the words that are most important. For others it is the beat, the cadence or the rhythm that speaks most to them.

I have heard people give answers to the Song-Slogan Question ranging from quotes from the *Bhagavad Gita*, through to Maori war cries, pulsating beats and "all you need is love", the song that Lennon wrote to mark the first global broadcast on television via satellite – a prelude to the connectedness we now take for granted. He said: "The only Purpose for us to do this show is communication so… here's my message." It communicates so much more than just the words.

Have a look at your song-slogan. Have a listen to it in your head. What does it remind you of? What are the thoughts and feelings you associate with it? What is it trying to tell you about your Purpose and how to access the most satisfying part of yourself? Could you develop a playlist around it? How would that affect you?

When I start a new project I try to get a feeling for its eight, nine, ten possibility… the one that will give the most value to the most people and then I "listen" for its unique vibe. I create a lot of development programmes for organizations using interactive theatre, which blends story, comedy and learning into an immersive experience. It's great fun, penetratingly insightful and highly energized. When I'm in "writing mode" I find myself listening to Madness. It has the bounce, the energy and a cheekiness in the tone and lyrics which help me translate my ideas to the page and then to the stage. Music is nutrition for the soul. What we take in comes out in other ways. For me, Madness, the sound of 80s Camden Town is irreverent, boisterous fun that secretes itself into a never-ending stream of gags and routines to tickle an audience and conjure the willingness to step on stage in front of their peers and take part in the action. If you haven't tried it, I thoroughly recommend it.

Find the vibe of the eight, nine, ten possibility, ingest it, watch it come out in other ways.

If your song-slogan centred around the words more than the rhythm and beat, perhaps it reveals your best advice to yourself and the words are serving as a guiding principle for you. We know the key guiding principles of many of the great individuals in history. Jesus said, "Do unto others as you would have them do unto you," while Gandhi surmised, "We must become the changes we seek in the world." Certain guiding principles define who we become and shape the quality of our actions.

When Tim, a participant, did the seven questions, here is what he put for the song-slogan:

> Watch your thoughts; they become words.
> Watch your words; they become actions.
> Watch your actions; they become habits.
> Watch your habits; they become your character.
> Watch your character; it becomes your destiny.

Most of what we write down is common sense. What changes life is when common sense becomes common practice. For Tim as for many others, a song-slogan can help us to articulate clearly our guiding principles. Reciting them can help us to become a more responsible, clearer-thinking, empowered and confident human being. We will have evolved.

Not only that, our song-slogan can impact others.

You know what it's like – you're in a bar or a restaurant, a song comes on that hits the spot and pretty soon the heads start nodding, people's feet are tapping and you see a few people mouthing the words in time with the lyrics playing through your head. The song has impacted the crowd.

When you look at coals in a fire they glow red. Each lump of coal gives its heat to the rest. Take a lump out of the fire and it goes dark again, replace it in the fire and the symbiosis is again triggered. The Song-Slogan Question carries the implication that somewhere, somehow, the people around us are going to pick up on the song-slogan of that near-invisible part of us I refer to as our "light-shadow"... so what is the impact you would most like to have on the people around you? Looking at your song-slogan, what can you learn about that? There's only one way to create the impact and that's to create the actions.

Often the subconscious mind will make suggestions to us in the form of music and lyrics as we go about our daily lives. These are often played in the background to our more conscious thoughts. Listen to the jukebox from time to time and see what it's suggesting.

Experiments

If you're starting a relationship or a project, about to go for a new job or embark on any other "new beginning", what would the song-slogan for it be? The eight, nine or ten iteration of it. Listen to it, learn it, sing it, love it and see how it changes your relationship to that thing.

Hold a picture of something you would like to "upgrade" in your life and imbue with the quality of your Purpose. Now, flow your song-slogan through it, like a river running through the landscape. Keep the song flowing until it feels as though the "thing" you are looking to upgrade has shifted.

If you are in a relationship, imagine you can hear your song-slogan in one ear and your partner's in the other. Allow the songs to mix in the centre of your mind and then see/feel them become perfectly harmonious in their melody and tempo. The rhythms may syncopate, the harmonies may change, even the style of music may be radically different... yet they find a balance together, each one enriching the other.

It's amazing what you can learn by changing the medium through which you interpret the world. A relationship seen through music can relate so much more than one expressed in words. It's all language and if it comes from a place of Purpose, it's all meaningful.

5. The World-Microphone Question

After answering the seven questions, people often remark that they had never before thought of themselves as "deep". More often than not they realize this is because they have never been asked to consider anything more profound than the day-to-day details of life. The World-Microphone Question asks us to articulate in a clear and concise way what we consider to be most important. The fact that our communication will appear on every piece of media on the planet encourages us to write our message in a clear and concise way that others will understand. As a result, we are unlikely to complicate things. Instead, we keep them simple. When people articulate meaningful things simply, they go deep.

Sarah, a particpant, found herself declaiming her world-microphone message. Its profound nature took her by surprise, so much so that she dismissed it at first as being "silly". Why do we do that? Only later when she shared it with her husband and others did she come to realize that it was exactly what she felt – and probably exactly what the world needs to hear. Here's what she said:

People of this Earth, you might think we are all so different; you might have feuds with your neighbours. You might think your way is the right way... But please, step back. Think! What is your Purpose?

Surely, to have a great time while you live on Earth? In that case *we all have the same Purpose*. Surely if we all work together we can make sure each of us creates a happy, healthy environment. All we have to do is give our best in what we know and respect the work of others. Be open-minded and learn from others, just as you can teach them.

Have faith, but only in the truth! The truth is, religion doesn't matter. God exists, whether you call him Jesus, Allah, the Big Bang theory or the sun.

The truth is we will never have a planet where everyone agrees with each other. However, we can agree to accept each other's different opinions, just as we have friends of different religions, cultures and ideologies.

The truth is that only by questioning ourselves constantly do we become aware of all this and work toward bettering ourselves.

Take some time out and think about the truth. Only then will we be a team.

Sarah grew up in a country where people of different religious faiths persecuted others. She also had a tendency to become highly stressed about certain events in her life. Her message showed her both the strength of her commitment to tolerance *and* served as a reminder to her to enjoy life, not to take it all too seriously.

Isn't it amazing that when we are asked a question about what you would say to the world if you had the chance, people come down to the core wisdom which, if applied, would change the course of humanity's trajectory. It is always the same. People's answers to this question are beautiful, bold, simple, kind and hopeful. In Shakespeare's *The*

Merchant of Venice, Portia says: "If to do were as easy as to know what were good to do, chapels had been churches and poor men's cottages princes' palaces. It is a good divine that follows his own instructions." We know what needs to change and we even know how to change it for the most part. What then turns intentions into actions? A brave few just do it. They don't spend too much time talking about it, they just get on with it and work out the details along the way. Most people change when it's convenient to do so... recycling when the bins are available, buying organic when it's in the supermarket, and so on. There are very few real leaders. People in positions of leadership in society are usually there because they want to be "leaders" not because they are championing a principle. The exceptions to this, such as Gandhi or Martin Luther King, Jr, are so much more effective than almost any "political" leaders in living memory. Why should this be so? Because they were led by their principles. It was their vision, their "world-microphone knowledge" that guided them. This inner conviction is connected to a greater source of wisdom, clarity and strength than anything most career politicians can muster.

If you choose to follow your principles you will almost inevitably become a leader. Not a political leader necessarily but a leader in the truest sense of the word. There's a lot of talk about leadership. There are thousands of books published about it each year. The truth is, though, leadership is not so difficult – having a vision, engaging people and forming strategy. It's much harder knowing what changes you want to make and not following your ideas through to completion than it is to embark on the journey of making the unknown known.

This question is also important in terms of where it occurs in the seven questions process. For the first time you are being asked: What do you stand for over and above yourself? The world-microphone is, to some, a great opportunity to say and give something meaningful to the world. For others, it is a frightening prospect to be asked to commit strongly to beliefs and to speak about them to a huge audience. Our messages are often the expression of values which are the essence of our humanity, respected throughout all cultures and ways of life.

The question is sandwiched between the song-slogan, which taps into your emotional life, and superheroes, which asks you about your hidden gifts and talents. Imbued with an emotional richness from the previous question, our world-microphone answer joins the eight, nine or ten places of our head and our heart. We are in our flow. What we say is true for us. So much so that it is this quality of truth that gives us the courage to speak to the world. This place, this integrity, this quality of commitment to personal truth is what sets us apart from Purpose-less people and moves us on from our old life. Such a fearless quality is intoxicating and magnetic. It makes us present to ourselves and that breeds... Presence.

Experiments

If you were to apply in your life the message you gave in answer to this question, what would you do? How might you make the global, local?

If you could turn your message into concrete actions, what would they be? How can you do them? How can you translate them into actions you can and want to carry out?

If you were to practise your world-microphone moment, how would you refine what you said?

If you were going to attach an image to your message, what would it be? Can you share it on social media? Are there quotes from your writing that stand out for you?

Who else feels the same? What do you think your friends would say in response to the question? How much do you think your answers would overlap?

Is your work in or out of alignment with your message? On a scale of one to ten? How could you pop it up a point?

And my favourite question: How could you make living your message great fun?

6. The Superhero Question

Superheroes have existed in one form or other in every society in the world and in every age. Greek gods, deities in the *Bhagavad Gita*, Thoth, Anubis, Thor, Taliesin and so on. They are archetypal and deeply intrinsic to our psyche. Perhaps they remind us that we are more than we appear.

When Alan answered the second part of the question ("If, in two weeks' time, you wake up in the morning and discover you have only one of the seven powers you wrote down, which one is it *most likely* to be?"), the power that jumped out at him from his list was "the power to be loved by all". He was reluctant to share this at first, feeling that the power he had chosen was a reaction to not feeling loved or appreciated. When we examined the answer to the last part of the question, about what you realistically do with that power, he gave a wonderful description about empowering others to believe in themselves and go beyond their limits. In other words, he wanted to be valuable to the whole through having given of his Purpose.

Does it really matter if the source of this choice was not feeling loved enough? I was the third child of four. As I grew up my mantra was "listen to me!" Obviously I did not feel listened to and that bred a plethora of thoughts, patterns and perhaps limitations. However... when I think about it... what did I do with this patterning? I became an actor... which I love. I learned about improvisation, delving deeply and creatively into the living moment. I became a storyteller and I have taught people to speak compellingly from their core. Feeling I was not being listened to may have forged these desires; however, there is a virtue to it.

I heard a wonderful story about a man walking home and seeing a chrysalis hanging from a branch on the tree outside his house. The butterfly struggles to break the bounds of its bonds. The man carefully plucks the chrysalis from the branch and takes it home. There he takes some nail scissors and carefully snips the edge of the surround. The butterfly immediately emerges onto his kitchen table and extends its wings to dry; however, it cannot fly. Why? Because it needed to push against the barrier of the chrysalis to build the strength it would need for flight.

There is nothing wrong with the stuff that has happened to us. We can't change it anyway. We can, however, change how we respond to it. Our past can be fuel for new, higher possibilities – or it can be a prison of our own consent. It's our choice. In this case Alan chose to use his superpower as a tool for emancipation and he loved that possibility. Love. That was his experience and the only thing that is real. His Purpose statement was: "I serve the Purpose of Enabling others to Fly."

The Superhero Question was when the penny dropped for Jenny. The first superpower she listed was the ability to change people's minds for their benefit. She instinctively felt that she did not need any other powers if this was possible, since it would allow her to achieve everything she wished. She put down six other powers just for her own enjoyment. In parts two and three of the question, asked which one power she was most likely to possess and what she would realistically do with it, she stuck with her original choice. She understood that what she really wanted to do with her life was to make a difference. There were many ways she could achieve this, and she chose to help people address their limiting attitudes and mindsets.

Jenny had taught aerobics for years. She has since begun training to be a facilitator and life-coach. Her Purpose statement was: "I serve the Purpose of Making a Difference."

So many people in modern society suffer from low self-esteem that it is practically an epidemic. It is said that when growing up, we hear, on average, "no" 17 times more than "yes".

"No. No. No. No. No. No. No. Stop that. Not now. Don't. Enough! No. No. No. No more. No. No... er OK, go on then. No. No. No."

Sound familiar? Obviously "no" is appropriate some of the time; however, when it becomes overbearing it can leave scars. People who grow up with little or no confidence in their abilities and talents start to lose them. The talents are still there but because they don't believe in them any more they stop indulging in them.

When baby elephants are being trained in India, one of their feet is chained to a pole stuck in the ground. They pull against it and pull against it but they can't get away. Eventually, they give up after concluding that the chain is unbreakable. As the elephant grows up it gets stronger and stronger. It could break the chain any time it wants to but it doesn't. Its belief is stronger than its reality. Eventually the pole is not even driven into the ground, and the elephant stays put.

Maybe such people have no idea of their strength or the depth and breadth of their abilities. Maybe there was no "category" for those people at school and no box to tick when it came to careers so they just stopped listening to a part of themselves that wants to live in the world.

Maybe by the time they came to work they had left those abilities alone for such a long time that they never factored into their choices. Like the elephant that includes the chain in all its plans for life.

Our gifts and talents are our modes of expression. Musicians express themselves through the music; dancers through movement; doctors through science, bedside manner or chemistry, or all of the above. Whatever our gifts and talents, they express us. Without honouring them we are a television production company that makes programmes but never broadcasts them, a comedian who never tells a joke or a chef who never steps foot in the kitchen. Knowing what our talents are and practising them is a way to know ourselves. It grows our confidence and self-esteem. If we simply do not give ourselves to them, we cut ourselves off from this source of vibrant esteem. Eventually, we can become so afraid to try anything outside our comfort zone that we let our world shrink.

I saw this phenomenon all the time when coaching public speaking. I met countless people who, due to their fear of standing in front of an audience, had carefully constructed careers designed to help them avoid the limelight. Often they were working way below their abilities for the "pay off" of not being seen. John Cleese famously said: "An Englishman's idea of a perfect life is to go from cradle to grave without the slightest hint of embarrassment." How many of us have curtailed our natural abilities to avoid some form of potential embarrassment?

Fear of our emotions... fear of what we might experience is the great dissipator of spirit. We have to realize that we can choose. Real choice, the kind of choice that marks a difference in our life, is not a once in a lifetime thing, it is a choice we remake and re-enact constantly. Does a beautiful wedding mean a great marriage? Of course not. A great marriage is made every day. Choice is repeated action.

The Superhero Question invites us into the room where our talents are stored... through the side door. It asks us, possibly for the first time, to consider what we would be like if we were an unlimited being. It places us in a situation where anything is possible and where we allow ourselves to have any talents we choose. The ones we choose are, therefore, important to us.

We often choose to have powers which are very close to our natural abilities. For example, a person choosing "telepathy" as a power may already be highly empathic, but may not fully trust their ability. Classic powers such as "flying" and "breathing underwater" often speak of a spirit of freedom seeking fuller expression in life.

The question also invites you to invent abilities. A lot of people create powers such as kindness and love-rays, emotional healing powers and the ability to change the fortunes of the world by affecting the environment or people's minds. The ability to stop war is a common theme.

The structure of the question asks us to draw answers from the realm of infinite possibility and apply them in the realm of actuality. Since the ideas of superheroes and superpowers are more acceptable to the subconscious mind than the conscious, it is the subconscious that answers the question. This means that when it is asked about the power it is "most likely" to have, it chooses the one closest to its understanding. Frequently this is an extension of an ability we already have, or one is brought to the surface that has been obscured through years of "reasonable" adult thinking.

When asked what we would realistically do with the power we are most likely to accrue, the question is again focusing our intent. Focused positive intent is the playground of our Purpose. Moreover, in answering the question, we begin to imagine ourselves as actually having this power. This imagination, in itself, starts to draw the latent ability closer to the surface. In answering the question as it stands we begin the process of embodying new abilities... We literally start to become a higher possibility of ourselves. This helps to complete the process, allowing our answers to the previous five questions to sink in and giving us the space to answer the seventh question – our Purpose statement.

Have you ever wondered if you had some special gifts or abilities? My experience of living on Purpose is that the moment we begin to live for something greater than ourselves we literally "expand" our capabilities. Things we thought we simply could not do, we learn. I come back to Gandhi again as an example. As you might know, when he first developed non-violent, passive resistance – drawing upon the ancient Indian tradition of *ahimsa* – it was a radical departure from the anti-colonial norm of opposition and it surprised the South African authorities. It was vitally important that he could communicate the essence of his approach effectively to those concerned. He had a great mind and a spectacular heart but was a poor public speaker. His modest character did not naturally suit the limelight. In fact it is said that when he was a boy, he was so shy that he used to run home from school so that he didn't have to talk to anybody. Does this sound like the kind of speaker who could evict the British Empire from its richest asset? He had a Purpose, however, which drove him beyond himself. He made sure that he learned and developed his speaking abilities to better serve this Purpose. The fact that India is independent is testament to his success

When the leaves fall from the trees in autumn it is because next year's leaves have started to grow within the branch. When they are ready for next year's growth, they push up against the existing leaf, cutting off the supply so that the leaf falls from the tree. The dying leaves create a rich mulch around the trunk of the tree, nourishing and enriching the soil and we are treated to a second summer of yellows and golds.

I believe we have no idea of what we are capable. I believe we need an excuse for new talents to grow. Serving a Purpose greater than ourselves is always going to extend and grow us,... which means that next year's leaves can come through and those will be our latent gifts and talents.

We need to have a cause for the talent to grow. Purpose is the cause.

Experiments

Life – version 2

This is a lovely exercise. Sit quietly and make sure you will be undisturbed for 15–20 minutes. Close your eyes and imagine you can see your whole life as a timeline. Go back to the very start and start living your life again as if all your talents came to the fore every day of your life. You can drift through your life fast or slow, go into detail or just see your talents as colours lighting up each day or week. Move through the years until the present moment. Feel these energized talents filling you, sinking into your cells. Now move them forward into the future, expanding your days and ideas.

Be watchful for particular moments in your history that will show themselves or seem more vibrant.

Your mind doesn't know the difference between what's real and what's imagined. See if your "present" feels different as a result of living your talents every day of your life.

Did you "see" any new or unexpected talents? Did the shape of your life change?

Notice also how you feel in the days following this exercise. It can have amazing effects!

Look at an area of your life that may be challenging at present. Ask yourself what talent you could have that would make this easier? More fun? An adventure? Find one example in your life of when you were good at this. Take that moment and plant it in the manure-filled fields of your current challenge.

You might have a difficulty around money. If you ask yourself for one example of when you were good with money, or had more than you needed, you might remember a moment when you won something as a child, found some money in a pocket of a jacket or landed a big deal. In your mind, take that moment and make it like a seed. Now have a look at your current situation. It might be a bit bleak, but that's great because it makes for greater potential. Plant your glowing seed and watch it grow and flourish. The more you enjoy the process the more it will flourish.

7. What is the Purpose I Serve?

Purpose is your essence and meaning expressed in the world. Knowing it and living it are the most important things you can do in this lifetime. Purpose brings happiness and fulfilment, and it enriches the world. When people arrive at their Purpose statements they tend to feel as if they have landed or come home. It is as if they are now being called by an ancient name they once had and they know themselves anew.

Many also want to know how the Purpose statement they've written fits in with those of other people, so below are some examples for you.

A client of mine called Rob is the CEO of a large company. The Purpose statement he arrived at was: "I serve the Purpose of Christianity in Action." Obviously this spoke to him on many levels, but he had no intention of foisting his spiritual beliefs and practices on others, so how would it affect the running of his business?

In the year following the discovery of his Purpose he replaced rules and regulations with a values-based system of management. This means that giving, respect, trust, listening and kindness now typify the nature of all his company's business practices. He has also introduced training to develop all staff, regardless of whether or not they are fee-earners for the firm. A man Rob works with suffered a bereavement which affected his work and relationship with clients. Through working with his Purpose, Rob chose to adopt a very supportive, compassionate way of dealing with the situation even though it could have proved risky, financially. It worked out very well for him, and both the colleague and the business are going from strength to strength. Rob feels that he is doing things "right" now. He feels as if he is being himself more than working to becoming "correct" in the eyes of others. His horizons have expanded, he spends more quality time with his family and he has blossomed as an individual.

Sometimes the effect our Purpose statement will have on our life is not obvious at first. For example, I took James, an actor, through the seven questions. The Purpose he arrived at – faithfully caring for those around him – spoke of his commitment to love and give to his friends and family. It touched him deeply and he knew that it was a true and driving force in his life. Over the following year he began to make significant changes in the direction of his career. He started his own theatre company and began running workshops, using theatre to develop and grow young people. He has proved an absolute natural and loves what he gives and gets from this new venture. It has brought him stability, success and meaning. The venture is not a literal translation of his Purpose in life, but it is a manifestation of the same qualities and values. Once he had discovered the "flavour" of meaning through his Purpose statement, he could not settle for anything less elsewhere. This has led him to express his talents where they are most meaningful. He then decided to become an actor's agent. He has been faithfully caring for a family of actors, helping them and him to ever-greater success.

Welcome to the Purposeful group of people of which you are now a part.

I am Peter,
I serve the Purpose of Inspiring Evolution.

I am Linda,
I serve the Purpose of Passionate Joy.

I am Richard,
I serve the Purpose of Marking and Sharing the Road to Happiness.

I am Vana,
I serve the Purpose of Compassionately Serving.

I am Martin,
I serve the Purpose of Being Truth.

I am Susie,
I serve the Purpose of Enabling Awesome Consciousness.

I am Belinda,
I serve the Purpose of Radiating and Celebrating the Power of Being.

I am Valerie,
I serve the Purpose of Enabling the Growth of Humanity.

The rest of this book is full of experiments and suggestions to help you take your answer to this last question and put it at the heart of your work, your play and, of course, your inner life.

Purpose Play

Plato, perhaps while dipping some warm pitta bread into a bowl of taramasalata, said: "I learn more about a man from an hour of play that from a lifetime of conversations." Play is the accelerated path to discovery, learning and integration.

Every mammal on the planet is born programmed to play. Why? Quite simply because the development of mammals, unlike reptiles, is not based primarily on instinct. Mammalian development is based on learning, and the fastest and most effective way to learn is through play. Ironically, it is also the least-used technique in schools and the training environment. In the sessions I currently run in the corporate world we now achieve in an hour of play what used to take us three days to achieve through classroom-based training. I have developed a methodology where people develop self- and collective-awareness and discovery through the exercises. I call this approach InterPlay (www.yesindeed.com).

In this chapter we are going to continue the "experiments" theme and look at a whole variety of ways you can experience your Purpose in ways that might baffle your conscious mind and delight your unconscious. Purpose is a process of discovery and engagement. So let's play...

"You only ever need to be a Master of Metaphor."

Aristotle

Everything that engages you with your Purpose, on both a metaphorical and literal level, makes it more tangible in our life. It starts to drive our actions and makes us "Purpose fit". These simple exercises help us engage with and feel your Purpose, on a number of different levels. The intellectual mind is predominantly based on knowledge, which is in the past or in concept. Our Purpose is bigger than us and beyond the known. It is a piste of discovery and therefore the natural interface with it is the imagination. Doing these simple exercises gives a fuller understanding of what our Purpose is in a way that we cannot get intellectually.

Experiments

There are no right or wrong answers to the following questions; just pop down your immediate response and see where it leads you. It's good fun, and helps the words come off the page and into your emotional reality. You don't have to do anything with your answers. They are there to give you a fuller, more definite feeling of the character of your Purpose. Some of the questions require you to jot something down on paper; some of them only ask you to think about the question. Do as many or as few as you like – whatever says "YES" to you at an eight, nine or ten...

If your Purpose were a...

meal, taste or flavour, it would probably be something like...
picture, it would probably be...
colour, it would be something like....
place, it would be...
sound...
song or piece of music...
smell...

What moments in films/books/articles/stories does it remind you of? Or a person – dead, alive or fictitious?

Where do you feel it in your body? What's the sensation like? Does that remind you of anything? Do you get that sensation from any other thoughts or activities? Which ones?

Many years ago I was running a presentation skills seminar. At one point there was a man at the front of the room. He was so nervous he could hardly look anyone in the eye or raise his voice to be heard at the back of the room. I asked him what he liked doing in his spare time. He told me he liked to race motorbikes. I said to him, "You mean to say that you are happy to take a corner at 120mph with your knee scraping against the tarmac, but standing in front of this group feels like a risk?"

"Yes," he said.

I said, "In that case, let's do both at the same time."

"What do you mean?"

We then walked through his presentation as if it were a racetrack. Each new point or change in topic was a bend in the road, each metaphor and anecdote was him overtaking an opponent, his final summary was him crossing the finishing line victorious. The whole process took no more than three or four minutes. He then spoke with verve and excitement. He engaged his audience at every turn, improvising as he went. In the end he stood his ground, strong and centred, and made his point. He had turned a corner and we all knew it.

There are different levels of knowledge, and among the most intense for any of us is that knowledge we feel in our bodies. We learn how to ride a bike when we're young; we haven't forgotten how to do so again once we're older. Our body "remembers" what to do. So it is with our Purpose. Integrating our Purpose on a physical level helps to fix the "idea" of what our Purpose is into our living, breathing reality. When we link new thoughts and knowledge with sensations and experiences we already know, we integrate them at a new level. It happens quickly and easily. Here are a few suggestions (see Experiments) as to how you might do that.

Experiments

If your Purpose was a stance or posture, it would probably be something like...

Stand or create the shape you feel your Purpose is likely to be. Become aware of your posture and what it is expressing in you.

How much does it say "YES" to you out of ten?

What would you have to do to move it up to a nine or ten?

If you were to translate that stance or posture into a hand movement or gesture, you would do something like...

Could you do this gesture discreetly in a way that nobody else would know what you were doing... undercover so to speak? If so, do it now.

Practise engaging with your gesture several times and see how much it reminds you of the quality of your Purpose. Change it or enhance it until it does.

Try doing this "undercover" gesture in meetings, before an interview or in any other challenging situations. Try it when your situations are not challenging and see what changes. How would you express the same quality while doing exercise? There is a lot of science behind the efficacy of triggering a physiological and psychological change through movement and posture (search Amy Cuddy on www.ted.com). Nobody will ever notice what you are doing, but you will know and that makes all the difference. As with all instinctive actions, simply repeating this gesture brings your Purpose back to the forefront of your mind. The more you bring your Purpose into your thoughts, feelings and actions the more you create from that place and the richer your results become.

If there is a physical object that speaks very strongly to you of your Purpose you may want to have it with you or in a prominent position to act as a reminder. Sometimes these objects just come to you out of the blue when you start to focus on your Purpose. The function of the object may not be anywhere near as important as its symbolism. If it feels new or different, pay special attention to what this symbol is trying to tell you. It is still an object, however. In and of itself it has no meaning. The meaning rests within you and is reflected through the subconscious mind in symbols. They are clues in the treasure trail of Purposeful pursuits.

I was away for the weekend with my wife and some friends and we were in a jewellery store. My friend was trying on a ring. I suggested that he bought it. He is a lawyer and said that although he loved it, he could never wear anything so daring at work. I said: "You have to try new things, mate... stretch the boundaries." At that moment he pointed out a highly unusual and distinctive ring and said, "Rich, try this". I have never worn much jewellery and this was so unusual I would never even consider trying it; however, the words "stretch the boundaries" were still on my lips so I had to concede. The man who owned the shop took the ring from a top shelf. It caught the sunlight as he lifted it. In one extraordinary motion he swooped it down onto my finger. We all gasped as it happened. We laugh about it now but it was an Excalibur moment. The ring has barely been off my finger since then. It speaks to me of so many qualities – more than I can account for – and has proved to be a marker point in my life.

Sometimes these things take you by surprise. Keep an eye out and see if anything comes to you.

Experiments

Try the following ways to activate and cultivate your Purpose.

Cook your Purposeful meal. Who would you naturally want to invite or include? How are they related to your Purpose? Have the dinner party and find out!

Go to a gallery or get a copy of your Purposeful picture. Where would you want to hang it? Where is it most appropriate? Why does it feel right there and not there?

See the film or read the relevant part of the book that reminded you of your Purpose. How does it make you feel? Do you walk or think differently afterwards? What part of yourself does this story reconnect you with?

What stories in newspapers, magazines and online speak to you of your Purpose.

Share your Purpose with others.

Think of five other ways to explore your Purpose and action those.

If there was one thing you could do today to explore your Purpose, it might be something like...

3

Purpose at Work

We spend 41–50 per cent of our lives either at work, including education, or commuting to it; 29 per cent asleep (presumably not at work); and the remaining 21–30 per cent of life is leisure time (weekends, holidays and retirement). The lion's share of our existence on this planet is related to work. How we engage with work is a big decision. If it's not Purpose-full it's Purpose-less.

Purpose-full work is when we can express and serve our Purpose through our work as well as our home, spiritual, family and other pursuits. I am fortunate enough to have been involved with many Purpose-full projects over the years. The profound effect they have on the people involved moves the whole idea of work into a different sphere. It becomes passionate endeavour.

There are some projects that come along where Purpose sits squarely at the heart. When people look back over their careers, it tends to be these projects which shine out for them because they hold deep personal meaning and, inevitably, have the potential to shape and affect many lives. Sometimes we seek and create these projects. At other times they seek us. As we start to live Purposefully we will probably both create and attract these kinds of projects. Here are some with which I have been involved. They have educated my spirit as well as my mind.

The European headquarters of NATO

In 2006 I had a call from a group of architects. They wanted to enter an international competition to design and build the European headquarters of the North Atlantic Treaty Organization (NATO). Could I help them with their bid?

I met with the team and we had some very interesting discussions. We talked about the difference between the function and the purpose of the building. What's the practical purpose of the building on a purely nuts and bolts level – in the way that the function of a car is to get from A to B regardless of the make, model, design or environmental impact? On another level, what does the building represent? What Purpose or ideal does it serve?

On a purely functional level the building was designed to house and coordinate the armed forces of the then 28 member states in the NATO alliance. However, there was also a provision to house key officials of states which were not members of NATO. In other words, an office block big enough to be a working home to all the armies of the world.

The Purpose, however, was something completely different. The nominated Purpose of the North Atlantic Treaty Organization was to protect member states by helping them coordinate their efforts against aggressors. Defence. Safety in numbers. Why were the new headquarters being built in Europe? If it was purely for NATO countries, why were potentially all the armies of the world to be gathered there in some form? And why now, at the start of the new millennium?

We discussed these questions in detail, which led to interesting conversations but at the end of our conjecture we were left with just that... conjecture. So, we had to decide what Purpose we nominated for this project. What would we like it to serve? The answer was simple: peace. The only possible beneficial reason for bringing the armies of the world together in one place is so that they do not have to fight to resolve issues. The design was done with that in mind. The lead architect Michel Mossessian (www.mossessian.com), a wonderful and hugely talented man, created a design of interlaced fingers symbolizing hands coming together across the world. We wrote our bid and made our presentations from this perspective. We won the bid. In 2017 work was completed on the site and the headquarters has been built with a dedication to peace. Had the nominated Purpose of the building been "defence" what would have changed?

Perhaps the design would not have been a symbol of cooperation. If one is designing from the perspective of defence, one ensures that people are not overlooked, that communal areas are discreet and people are discouraged from meeting or overhearing others, and so on.

If one is designing for peace, shapes are rounder and more generous. Light and green areas become more important. There is a focus on communal areas, collective discussion and both informal and formal meetings. Colours are softer and people are encouraged to connect with greater openness.

Peace connects. Defence separates. Purpose changes everything.

The Maitreya Project

Another extraordinary project I had the privilege to be involved with already had a well-defined Purpose. A client of mine, another architect, won an international competition to design and build the Maitreya Project. Buddhists believe that the successor to the current era's Shakyamuni Buddha is Maitreya, the Buddha of the Future, who will appear in this world as a saviour figure during a coming dark age for humanity when Buddhism is no longer practised. The Maitreya Project will build, in India, the tallest statue in the world, which will also be a working building, clad entirely in bronze so that he will glow golden in the sun, and is designed to last 1,000 years. His head will be above the clouds for part of the year and one will be able to hold meetings in the different *chakra* points of Maitreya Buddha's body. The throne on which the colossal Maitreya Buddha will sit is the size of a world championship sports stadium. The back of the statue is to be made of 250,000 different effigies of the Buddha in glass, so that when the sun shines in the sky in 500 years' time it lights up the prayer hall.

The Purpose of the Maitreya project is to be a permanent reminder to humanity, even in its deepest despair, that there is a higher possibility we can strive for: darkness is not the end, it is the light.

The Purpose of the project was clear, compelling and inspiring beyond imagination. The client was a Buddhist organization that wanted to ensure the construction process was in accordance with its spiritual principles. There were no towns or cities near the proposed site, which meant that there was no hospital for the thousands of workers needed for the build. How could we construct field hospitals to care for injuries in a way that was sustainable and potentially more advanced than any military triage facility.

I was working with the architects, construction engineers and the team as a whole to help them to embrace multi-dimensional creativity and to think in new and paradigm-shifting ways. It was extraordinary. Senior architects, who had designed signature buildings, would say they were willing to design mere toilets and door handles just to work on the project. What interested them was the Purpose of the project and how they could devote themselves to it. Purpose, it seems, is far more fulfilling than any task; knowing what our work is for rather than the work itself.

The European Union

Seven days before the UK's Brexit referendum I started working with the European Union (EU). My commitment is to peace. Between people this is cultivated and maintained through connection, communication and symbiosis. The same is true for countries. Europe has enjoyed its greatest period of prolonged peace since the inception of the European Community in the 1950s. Like everything there are improvements and upgrades that can be made, but the fundamental principles – of strength in unity, tolerance and mutual cooperation – lead to the betterment of society... connection, communication, symbiosis.

The Purpose I nominated for my work with the EU was "Unity in Community". The essence of this statement is that the generation of a thriving community at the height of its effectiveness acts as a conduit for the same enlightenment throughout its associated bodies. In other words, to create a movement of higher possibility, which spreads like a virus across the EU bodies to the member states and beyond. The EU originally hired me to deliver some communication training. The Purpose was something I held within. I did not mention it in any way, formally or informally.

After my first training session I was sitting outside enjoying a summer drink and I met a woman who was heading up the EU's work on epigenetics, the study of the physical evolution of the human species. "What's epigenetics?" I asked. She explained that only about 5 per cent of our gene pool is active and that occasionally another 0.5 per cent or 1 per cent becomes activated. When that happens people undergo radical shifts; some for better, some for worse. On one level people can lose all their resistance to diseases or become massively intolerant to foodstuffs. On another level they can become extraordinarily resistant to extreme temperatures. It was the X-men. Epigeneticists therefore study the factors – food, stress, pollution, our thinking, population densities – that lead dormant genes to become expressive ones.

She said that with the exception of a couple of scientific bodies with the size and resources of her own only the big pharmaceutical companies and some universities were doing epigenetic research, but that most of the universities couldn't publish their work because they are sponsored by big pharma.

I love corporates. I have worked with them for years and met some fantastic people and done some wonderful work, but their Purpose is essentially to work in their own interests first and in the general interest second, if at all. The EU's purpose is to work first and last for the greater good. Do we really want to leave that to the organizations which work for their own interests? Don't we want a second opinion on their findings?

It became clear to me that the value of organizations such as the EU cannot be measured by the short timescales discussed in pithy soundbites, tweets and newspaper headlines, or the voting cycles of national governments. This value extends way beyond a single lifetime. We have to think of the long-term betterment of humanity more than short-termism.

I committed deeply to the EU and my purpose for it that night. Since then my communication training and development work has "organically" spread throughout the EU bodies. I have helped leaders develop radical new approaches to their work, their teams and the public at large. We are developing projects which could fundamentally shift the behavioural operating system of global bodies, and I initiated a programme to "win back 20 per cent of people's time every week" (www.timehacks.life). In a body of 500 people this equates to over a year's worth of time every week. It is literally a life-giving project and is reverberating throughout my other client groups.

The Purpose gave rise to the projects and those projects are spreading virally.

Beer with Purpose

Can beer really change the world? Well, it already has. Beer was one of the principal reasons humanity changed from being hunter-gatherers to settlers. Getting enough food to eat was always a challenge. Hunting was hard work and foraging would only bring in so much. One day someone drank the water where grains had fermented. It fed them and it felt good. People realized that they could live more easily within reach of this foodstuff and eventually learned how to repeat the process, changing the shape of society.

So, what has this got to do with Purpose?

My company YES was approached by one of the largest brewers and distributors of beer in the world. It produces over 200 million bottles of beer every day, which is more than the populations of Brazil and Russia combined. Every year it produces six times more bottles of beer than there are people on the planet. How they treat the land, their workers, local communities, create packaging, print for their labels, sell to distributors and what they put into their products and therefore into their consumers, affects billions of people every day.

The company wanted to help its people "do the right thing"... make decisions which benefit their people, consumers, their reputation and the planet as a whole and to think further than process. In essence they asked us to create an ethics programme that could be shared and adopted by over 70,000 employees in virtually every country in the world.

We had to completely rewrite the book. Working globally meant that the programme had to be delivered through media. Creating a change in mindset means involving and engaging people not just "telling them stuff". Working with people who ranged from the most technologically enabled to those without broadband meant that the programme had to work on paper (through PDFs) as effectively as online. We had to use graphics to get around language barriers and an interactive story to trigger conversations.

We created interactive scenarios by means of a comic book-style infographic interface, which team leaders could use as a basis for discussion and generating ideas with their teams. A "mindset funnel" moved people's thinking into the ethical zone and a gamified learning environment was developed in which people's suggestions would come back to them in follow-up scenarios. Essentially, this meant creating an interactive soap opera on paper that incorporated the suggestions and ideas of 70,000 people in real time.

This approach is now being adopted by other global operators and is proving to be a step-change in mass communication and digital engagement.

Purpose is the matriarch of invention.

The place to tap

There is a great, apocryphal, story about a large steamboat that broke down in Sydney harbour in the early part of the 19th century. The captain called out an engineer, who arrived at the boat carrying a little black bag. When he went down to the engine room he began knocking on the pipes and smelling the air. Eventually, he made his way to the far corner of the room, opened up his bag and took out a little hammer. He tapped it three times on one part of a small pipe and put it back into his bag. "Fire up the engines," he called. The engines roared into life. He gave the captain his invoice for US$5,000. "Five thousand dollars!" protested the captain. "How dare you charge me so much? All you did was tap a pipe." "Yes," replied the engineer. "If you notice, I have only charged you five dollars for tapping the pipe. I charged you $4,995 for knowing where to tap." One seemingly small shift can have a huge impact. Purpose is that small shift... personally, interpersonally and professionally.

Purpose is the place to tap. It has sponsored more innovation than just the desire to innovate. The scale Purpose invites is so much larger than the immediate deliverables that it becomes the root cause of evolution. Businesses and corporations require scale. The infusion of Purpose into what they do is like nutrition for the soul.

My experience in creating and delivering Purposeful programmes in this environment is that people just want more. They don't know why or what it is exactly that they want more of – it's like a flavour they didn't know they loved until they tried it.

People today are largely starved of Purpose in the workplace. We have to find ways to bring it in – for our sanity, enjoyment, for the sustainability of the planet... and for the fun. We must become Purpose-full rather than remaining Purpose-less. There are six main areas where we can stimulate Purpose-full thinking and then apply Purpose-full action in the workplace. The six are career choices, leadership, adjusting to change, being time effective, making meetings matter and managing power play. The following section explores these six areas.

Careers

If work takes up nearly half our lives, how can we apply Purpose to career choices?

I always knew what I wanted to do. I was lucky that way. However, most of the people I grew up with didn't. Where do people go for guidance on the jobs they are going to choose? Careers advisers? Career guidance is not focused on what drives us fundamentally as human beings – the achievement of our deep-seated fulfilment and the exploration of our talents; instead, it is focused on ticking the boxes identified by our education, which in itself is a generalized compartmentalization of knowledge rather than ability. Education, for the most part, is the commoditization of human intelligence based on the idea that people grow up to serve the status quo as opposed to evolving it according to their unique possibility. Careers advice takes generalized intelligence and fits it into even more generalized boxes. And that's supposed to be a route to happiness?

If young people knew their Purpose before making career choices, it would change everything. Not only their jobs, but their relationships, how they are as parents (people who are more fulfilled make better role models). It affects how much we drink, smoke or take drugs – if we do not need to compensate for our lives, our habits change. Of course, our perspective and what we want from life change over the years. We can revisit our Purpose at any time to make fresh choices. What is important is that we make big life choices in line with what we hold most meaningful.

If people understood their Purpose before changing jobs, it would give them a renewed drive or focus and it would increase their chances of success. If people within jobs were connected to their Purpose they would simply not create the levels of dysfunction that currently appear in the workplace. Most people are asleep. Somnambulists. Why would they bother to wake up for anything less than thrilling?

The very first training programme I learned how to deliver was in the field of outplacement – working with people who had lost their jobs. We had a fantastic success rate – 90 per cent of people found new jobs within six months with equal or better pay. Over the years I have helped many people through career transitions. I often do the following exercise (see Experiments) with people who have done the seven questions and are looking to apply that in a job:

Experiments

Make a list of 20 jobs that would express your Purpose at an eight, nine or ten out of ten.

As you make your list, be aware that new jobs will spring to mind, especially when you have gone past number 13 or 14. Insist on writing down 20 jobs.

If you find this hard to do, try this version: If you had 20 lives but the same Purpose, what jobs might you want to try?

Circle your top three or four and see how you can combine them in much the same way as we answered the Tombstone Question.

If combining the jobs does not give you what you want, ask what qualities these jobs give you – creativity, independence, travel, financial security, connection with people, leadership... Can you think of one job that will give you these qualities?

Changing job

In a similar way to the career guidance path, when people change jobs they almost always look for what they can do rather than what they would love to do. Remember, it's 41–50 per cent of your life. This is not a rehearsal. Wake up and go for what you love, otherwise by the time you do you will wish that you had started years ago. Why wake up to the game you most want to play when you're halfway through the second half? Why not play your heart out from the beginning?

I recently met with a man who had been my manager when I was 16 years old and had a holiday job. We have kept in touch over the years. He was the director of a large organization (employing over 15,000 people) but the company had been bought out and although he had secured a decent settlement he still needed to work. He wasn't sure what to do, how to go about finding a new job or even exactly what he wanted to do after all this time.

As we spoke I asked him lots of questions. I was looking for two things in his answers:

1. Repeated patterns – similar situations or ways in which he talked about limitations or opportunities.
2. When the "lights came on". At moments and in response to certain questions, he lit up. This told me more than any information or data he might surrender.

I noticed that whenever I asked him about what he really wanted to do, he would turn the question into what kind of a job people would see him suited for, or ask what he could do at his age? I kept on reframing the question until he talked about what he loved and found thrilling rather than what he thought was "realistic". Realistic is simply a belief paradigm. Was it realistic that the man who became Colonel Sanders could start Kentucky Fried Chicken in his 60s with his last few dollars when he had failed miserably at everything he had ever tried? Was it "realistic" for Sylvester Stallone to sell his script for *Rocky* and play the lead role when he had just sold his dog for £25 so that he could eat? Was it "realistic" for JK Rowling to expect to become richer than the queen while sitting in a cafe in Edinburgh to keep warm writing a children's novel? None of these stories are "realistic" but they are examples from real life. Our beliefs determine our reality and they are formed and reinforced minute by minute, moment by moment. Our doubting voice, although – ironically – it speaks with great confidence, knows nothing. It has no greater handle on "reality" than your positive mind. My friend's doubting voice was saying things like:

"Nobody will hire you, you're too old."

"Your experience is so niche it can't apply to another company."

"There are so few jobs available for you."

"You just won't be able to find the jobs. They won't be advertised and people will hire from within the company."

You get the idea.

I asked him how his doubting mind had become such an expert? "When you're asleep, does your doubting mind go on the Internet and research how likely it is for someone with your skill-set to find a new opportunity? How does it know so much?" I then asked him: "If your doubting mind was a human being instead of a voice in your head, would you want to hang out with them? Would you like them? Would you trust them? Would you want their advice?" He said, "No way." I said, "Well in that case, tell it where it can go." He laughed and the point was made.

We then talked about which elements of his work he loves and has always loved... the parts he would do for free or would look for in any job in which he found himself. All the lights came on. The sunshine of his enthusiasm chased away the clouds of doubt and he spoke animatedly about working with people, solving problems and the trusting, human contact he enjoys with clients. From this conversation sprang a host of ideas and people for him to contact. One of which has led to a new and bold opportunity. The ideas come from the clarity and the enthusiasm, not from the doubts. Love breeds love. Doubt breeds fear.

Yes, we have to be practical in life. We have to look for work. We have to earn money and there is a pragmatic way of going about things; however, does that mean that we also have to ignore what says "YES" to us most? Is that really life? What if our choices were far stronger than we thought they were? What if our possibilities were far greater? What if we can be the people we want to be instead of compromised views of ourselves?

Here's a great exercise if you want to have a fresh look at your work. You can also apply this same exercise to any number of other practical considerations.

Experiments

Take a piece of paper and write three pages non-stop. Start each sentence with "I would absolutely love to..." – or, if it feels more juicy for you, use expletives. See what comes out. Don't edit, be correct or feel like you have to show this to anyone. It is to reveal yourself to yourself – in fun. After you have done the exercise, look for eights, nines and tens and repeated themes. See how you can combine to enrich.

Purpose and uncertainty

I was called into a big bank in the City of London at the point where they were about to be bought by a bigger bank. The human resources people were mindful of the fact their people were going through a great period of uncertainty and wanted to do something positive for them. The City is a fairly cut-throat environment in which people tend not to show how they feel, let alone admit vulnerability. To succeed in helping people meant finding a way through cynicism and a disassociation of emotion without meeting people face to face. This gave birth to what I call the "Frictionless Argument". Which goes like this...

If you stay in your current job during this period of uncertainty, does that mean that you will be safe and secure? If you jump ship now and join a new company are you guaranteed to be safe and secure? How do you know that there won't be a "reshuffle" there too?

Where does *real* security come from? Does it come from having a job or being valuable? If it comes from being valuable, how do you grow your value as a human being? The only intelligent answer to this question is: by growing myself.

Growing oneself means cultivating Purpose, skills development and a resilient attitude. With these three attributes one becomes infinitely more attractive as a candidate. It also means that in the moment of uncertainty, instead of retreating and battening down the hatches, one extends oneself and grows through the uncertainty to certainty.

This, to me, is how people shape their destiny within a job. They choose to grow themselves, in all things, in all ways. Personal development and professional development are the same thing.

Being your own boss

People often say to me that they tolerate their job but it does nothing for them and they wish they were their own boss. I say to them, "You are always your own boss. Even when you have a boss, you never surrender your personal autonomy." Rubin "Hurricane" Carter was a middle-weight boxer who was arrested for triple murder in 1966 during the height of the civil rights movement. Despite people campaigning on his behalf, he served a life sentence. He never surrendered his autonomy, even in prison ignored by the authorities. The same is true for Nelson Mandela and a host of others. Our choice for dignity – in work, in life – is our choice. It can belong to no other. Like making eight, nine or ten choices on a five, six or seven island our circumstances may not be what we wish but how we face them is entirely our own. That is self-determination. That is responsibility. That is freedom.

You are always your own boss.
Your life is important.
Your career is the lion's share of your life.
It is a perfect vehicle for your Purpose if you choose.
You choose every day.
Would you "sell" ten years of your life to boredom just so that you could make ends meet?
20 years?
It's now.

Leadership

There is an ancient guiding principle apparently championed by the Celtic kings – "Lead by serving, serve by leading". This sums up the essence of leadership at its highest. I have met many leaders in business, industry, show business and politics and most of them tend to behave as if they are the most important person in the room. However, for those whose focus is Purposeful leadership, the opposite tends to be true. Purposeful leadership is when Purpose is the boss and the role of leadership is to take decisions and enable the people around them to achieve their greatest potential; to be this kind of leader is to be a facilitator and an enabler. Whereas traditional leadership tends to be about control, Purposeful leadership is about empowerment.

There's a fabulous game I play with groups that highlights admirably people's preconceptions about leadership. People sit in circles and close their eyes. One person is tapped on the shoulder and a moment later everyone opens their eyes again. The person touched then becomes "the leader". They will not do anything in particular to draw attention to themselves, they will simply *be* the leader. We then have a minute or two where everyone has to work out, without talking, who they think the leader is. Each person (including the "leader") then points to their chosen person.

We play the game twice. In the first round I touch nobody on the shoulder. In the second round I touch everybody on the shoulder. The difference in atmosphere and behaviour between rounds one and two is astonishing. In the leaderless, people are open, they look at each other, pay attention and are outwardly focused; there is laughter and plenty of smiles. In the second round, there is little or no connection between people. They expect others to be looking at them. All laughter and smiles cease and the atmosphere becomes severe. When we reveal who the leaders were or weren't there is a lot of laughter and discussion. People start to identify the unconscious traits they associate with leadership... seriousness, responsibility, and so on.

I have been playing this game for 20 years. The results have always been the same, regardless of the nationality, style of organization or culture. People seem to associate leadership with solemnity and feel implicitly that it makes them more important than others and thus should elicit greater respect and deference from the people around them. When I ask people if these qualities actually help leaders become more effective they say "no" categorically.

The spectrum of control and empowerment

On the control side of this spectrum is the idea that rigid structures and measures reduce risk and enable greater results – that the "higher-ups" in the organization know more and that any initiatives created at the "lower levels" need to be sanctioned through lengthy processes. The upshot of this is that significant new ideas are actioned by only about 4 per cent of the population of an organization, and that people are discouraged from taking responsibility and therefore, ironically, become less capable leaders as they progress. The emphasis of the control mindset is the elimination of risk through human error and lack of initiative.

On the empowerment side of the spectrum is the notion that people want to do their best and that extending their abilities is more fulfilling, rewarding and desirable. There is a release of control, trusting in the abilities and motivation of others to work in favour of the whole. There is greater risk and there is also greater reward. Empowered cultures evolve faster than those governed by control. Why? Because someone who wants to control others is in the business of limiting possibilities and spends significant time and resources monitoring and sanctioning. That's risk aversion and it moves at a slow pace, like someone creeping along an icy pavement.

Empowered people are not threatened by the people around them reaching their potential; they actively encourage it, knowing that the more the person next to them progresses, the more they will progress also. Rock climbing is the perfect metaphor for this... we spend time securing our partner so that they can climb higher. Then, in turn, they secure and help us. Together we get to the top. Empowered cultures release more ideas into the mix, have a greater sense of energy and personal responsibility and break the moulds of the status quo. They are less focused on hierarchy and more on getting things done and enjoying the journey.

It is rare that the extremes of any doctrine are the optimum; we always need a balance.

We see the same dichotomy played out in global politics. Pick a world leader and place them on the imaginary control–empowerment spectrum in your mind. If they are heavily on the control side, you will probably see their rhetoric being echoed verbatim by all the people around them. They tend to speak in absolute terms, tend to deal with opposition aggressively, trying to win at every turn and the only ideas that are actioned tend to be their own. If you place them more on the empowered side, they will likely be warmer, have a better sense of humour, feel more spontaneous, surround themselves with people who speak their mind and will speak more in terms of "we" than "I".

Which of the two would you like to invite back for dinner?

Which of the two would you want to spend more time with?

Which of the two would you prefer to be like?

Most leadership dysfunctions stem from a belief that having status somehow makes us better than someone else. I grew up as an actor. It has shaped the way I see the world. Every role someone plays in life or in art is, to me, a playground and path of experimentation. I have always found myself sitting around tables in boardrooms wondering "What I would have to think, say or do 'to *play* you, truthfully'?" Without knowing it, I was using all my skills and craft as an actor to empathize completely and without judgement. It's great fun and extremely revealing. I can't help wondering why businesses are not more like theatre companies. Bit of a strange concept, really. I mean... Theatre companies are normal. What I mean by that is that no matter how old an actor is or what part they are playing they are inherently equal to any other actor no matter how young. You get some young star who comes in because he's in a soap opera and has just done a Levi's advert and he's going to bring "the young crowd in"... "make Hamlet relevant to the Instagrammers because they've got the hots for him". Actually, he's saying "to be or not to be" and the audience is busy tweeting "these jeans or those jeans... that is the question". The old actor probably worked with Olivier, Sir Ralph Richardson and Sir John Mills – but so what, his equity is actually less than the young buck who's on standby for the new Kellogg's campaign. That's the way it works. On stage the old guy is playing Claudius or something and he's all status and crowns surrounded by genuflecting serfs, but back in the green room (the room offstage where you relax between scenes) he's tea and gardening.

Translate that back into the boardroom and the young guy's got a ten-minute presentation slotted into a packed day of data, charts and politically motivated Machiavellian machinations. (That's got to be a triple score for alliteration, right?) So, he's sweating, thinking that he has to impress them. A nod from people at that table and... his stock goes up, his words become weighted with gold in his conversations with peers: "So then I challenged them, 'the question is not, does the index show our diversity alignments, it's more how do we leverage this cross-functionally?'"... Pause for awe. "I got a nod and a half-smile from the 'chief exec'. Kerching. I am effing made!"

So what's funny about that? Two things really. The first is that the people around the boardroom table more often than not actually see themselves as better in some way than the guy sweating over his PowerPointed audition... like royalty bequeathing their smiles and their time. They play the role full-on... As full-on as the old guy playing Claudius. The only problem is, they don't realize that they are going on stage; for them it's real. The old actor doesn't think that people should treat him like Claudius in the green room. He knows he's just another guy. The chief exec, or chief investment officer or chief management leadership executive officer director, doesn't. Why? That's the second thing... Everybody around them thinks they're royalty too. They say that the royals think that the world smells of fresh paint; why wouldn't they? They must think that everybody lives on best behaviour. You're not allowed to touch the queen's hand? Seriously? Not allowed to touch her hand? As if... what? There must be some separation for her status to be retained? It's insane.

So, the chief management leadership executive officer director doesn't realize that they're on stage... Because the young actor (Hamlet) treats him as Claudius. Hamlet doesn't realize that he's on stage either because Claudius is acting like a king or queen and nobody breaks character. So, all the world's a stage that's forgotten there's a green room. What a nightmare! Can you imagine *being* Hamlet and not realizing that you are in fact *playing* Hamlet? You spend your whole life gazing into your navel going: "What should I do? Actually I know what to do but I can't do it. I don't know. I know but I don't know. I

mean should I?... Maybe... Perhaps... Not sure... I mean... Whatever..."
Actually, I know lots of people like that and it is a nightmare.

The green room is where everyone's normal again. I remember playing Tybalt in *Romeo and Juliet*. I'd just had this great fight, taking on two Montagues at once, prancing around the stage in my Elizabethan finery, feeling like Ethan Hunt in tights, and scarpering when the prince came on stage, played by an actor called Paul Sirr, who had this HUGE voice:

"Rebellious subjects, enemies to peace,

Profaners of this neighbour-stained steel –

Will they not hear?..."

Everybody on stage was immediately muted by his commanding tone, frozen by the authority of the voice. Somewhere in the distance a dog barked.

Ten minutes later we're sitting next to each other in the green room. He opens his paper to read his horoscope and waits for Mercutio to die. He's real. He doesn't think he's the prince. It's fun playing him for a while but then he comes off stage. He's just who he is and status has no play. It's just a convention we buy into so that we can see more about reality through the lens of a fantasy. It's a fiction in the same way that the boardroom is a fiction. The work isn't, but the status is. All status is. It's the fiction that keeps the fiction of the world standing. One good look at it and the fiction collapses... like the emperor with no clothes and no fool nearby. So people keep propping it up. As Bill Hicks said, every once in a while a person comes along who reminds us that this [the world] is all a ride, that we're making the whole thing up, and... "We kill those people". People are invested in status because they think it's better to be "better than" – but to become "better than" they have to be "worse than". And when they're "better than" they have to make others "worse than". So better than is worse than and worse than is better than other worse thans... And vice versa. It's a fictional merry-go-round. Except that it's not very merry. More marred than merry.

Knowing who you are doesn't need to be "better than". Can't be worse than because who you are is unique. There's no merry-go-round – it's all green room. We're free to go on stage and play a part for a bit and then come back to newspaper horoscopes. Everyone knows that the world doesn't smell of fresh paint. It smells of the world... and what could be better than that? Don't buy into the fiction. Live in the real world. It's much better than...

Change

Evolution is out of control.
Masters of change are people who embrace the unknown.
Purposeful people live for something greater than themselves.
Which means they live beyond the known and at the edge of possibility.
Now is your time.

An airplane is off course 99 per cent of the time. It is being pushed by winds, updraughts and turbulence, and as a result is in a constant state of flux. Why then do planes not get lost? Because they are constantly taking compass and navigation readings in relation to their destination. Being 99 per cent off target is fine as long as we continue to adjust. That's the value of Purpose in times of change. Purpose does not change. Everything else does.

This is more important now than ever before.

The rate of change in the outside world far exceeds the rate of change within organizations. Industry leaders can be made and broken in a few short years (think of Google and Blackberry). Culture-change programmes, aimed at instigating a big change in the way people think and behave, which used to happen every nine years or so in the 1980s and 1990s, are now constant. The world's socio-economic tectonic plates are shifting seismically on a daily basis. The fifth-biggest economy in the world wants to leave the EU. Is that going to affect business? Of course it is. People cannot predict market forces six weeks away and yet are still trying to develop three-year plans. Nobody knows what's going to happen but they continue operating as they did when the world was predictable. Heads down, keep going, hope for the best. It doesn't work. It's not going to work and... it's only going to get more intense. The rate of change in the outside world far exceeds the rate of change within organizations. That's unsustainable.

Millions of years ago when brontosauruses walked the earth, food was so plentiful that they effortlessly grew bigger and bigger. After a while they were so large that they could not generate enough energy to digest their food and they started eating different foods so that the enzymes would break down the food in their stomachs. The result was that they got bigger and the new diet could not cope with their mass. They had to start eating rocks and gravel so that the food could be broken down inside their stomachs. No prizes for guessing what happened next – they grew larger and larger. At their apex they were the size of a three-storey house and at full speed – a sprint with a following wind – they could travel at 4mph, the same as our average walking speed. At that pace, it does not take a genius to work out that should anything happen – a new predator or a change in the environment – by the time they have turned their heads to see what the commotion is about, they will have been wiped out. Slow-motion responsiveness.

Long-drawn-out decision-making, meetings that clog up the diary but go nowhere, 40-slide presentations when three slides would do, lengthy documents and cc'ing 15 people in on emails are all symptoms of brontosaurian behaviours. They are all attempts to mitigate risk, manifested as systems of control. They make good sense up to a point but there's a problem, a limitation… and it is that "control" doesn't like change – it can't abide chaos. The casualty of this is a dearth of creative freedom. Our creativity, our capacity to innovate, solve problems and come up with new solutions to old problems, is absolutely essential if we want to continue to thrive in constantly changing environments. How can we possibly evolve without it? Could you surf a wave while keeping your body rigid? Growing creativity does not come from systems of control but from facilitation and empowerment.

People don't like change.

Actually, when you really look at it, it's not change that makes them fearful, it's their assumptions about the future, but that's a different story. People born into systems of control – and by that I mean traditional management and leadership – normally respond to change by reapplying aspects of their old model and hoping for the best. We were working with an organization recently that had experienced year-on-year growth of 11 per cent for the previous five years. Suddenly the market changed for them. New competitors came to the fore along with legislation changed in respect of their products. Nobody knew how to deal with the shift. What did they do in response? They pretended everything was under control; they kept bashing away at the same set of problems using the same solutions that they had always used, smiling on the outside and panicking on the inside. This was a major international organization with highly intelligent people. And even though the workforce was young they simply did not know how to change. Micro-adjustments to the status quo felt radical to them. People simply do not have "embracing change" as a default setting in their personal operating system. Yet.

Our fundamental choice in response to the inevitable waves of change determines our path of evolution. Change comes in waves. Waves come in sets and the sets are now constant. Surely if we were going to be in the sea for a long time with waves crashing over us, we would want to learn how to ride them, wouldn't we? What's the alternative? Have each wave crash down on us and hope for the best? Suffer or surf, that's our choice.

The three strands of change

There is a missing link in the way organizations think about change. There are three strands to any change programme:

1. Strategy.
2. Processes.
3. Mindsets and behaviours.

None of these is optional.

If you launch a change in strategy but your processes cannot cope with the new, the strategy will inevitably fail. If we change behaviours but the strategy and processes remain the same, what, realistically, is going to change? Changes in strategy and process without a shift in mindsets and behaviours cannot get us where we want to go. It's like designing a fabulous new car. It may have a state-of-the-art engine and a great interior but it has no wheels. Nice but no cigar. Because none of the three strands is optional, they must all evolve in concert with each other. Or to put it another way, if you build a brand new school (Strategy) and you provide the pupils with new IT systems (Processes) but the teacher walks into the classroom and continues to teach (Behaviours) in exactly the same way as they did in the previous school, what, in real terms, has changed?

There are two reasons why mindset and behavioural change is not more widespread. First, most organizations don't know how to measure those and only tend to value what they know how to measure. Second, leaders don't understand how to achieve a widespread mindset and behavioural change. There is a difference between wanting change and wanting to change. For many people, wanting to change is uncomfortable.

The truth is, though, that it is now starting to become more uncomfortable not to change than to change. We've come as far as we can in an organizational model derived from the armed forces and we find ourselves on the brink of the next level of evolution. When the tectonic plates of the earth move it is rigid structures that crumble, whereas the flexible survive and thrive. As Darwin said, "...it's not the fittest or the strongest of a species that survives, but the ones most adapted to change".

So do we become extinct like brontosauruses or is there a next step in our evolution?

Five principles for a murmuration of Purposeful people

Have you ever seen a murmuration? (Look up "starlings, murmuration" on YouTube.) Thousands of starlings twisting and turning in unison, creating a wondrously evolving cloud that avoids predators and obstacles? Ever wondered how it is possible that these birds can create self-evolving systems of a complexity and agility that far outstrips anything achieved by human beings... and yet they have brains the size of peanuts? What if our organizations, public and private, could operate with this level of dynamism, harmony and responsiveness to the ever-changing work environment? Is this some pipe-dream that we share in HR circles over a particularly well-brewed latte or is it a survival necessity? To my mind, it's the latter not the latte. Could a Victorian steam train hold together at the speed of modern bullet trains? Unlikely. Can the way we operate as organizations formed mostly in the 1980s and 1990s hold together in today's quantum-accelerating environment? No way.

A murmuration of thousands of starlings can evolve and transform as one at incredible speed. The macro-organism they form has an extraordinary and complex capacity to change that is based on five simple, self-organizing principles – cohesion, alignment, proximity, obstacle and predator awareness – which help them to avoid threats, share information, identify opportunities, learn from each other and feed more effectively. In other words, they enjoy safety, security, increased productivity and they evolve in sync with the forces that govern their environment. This, for me, is the perfect metaphor for Purposeful people operating together for the greater good: a murmuration of Purposeful people. In the human organizational environment the five equivalent principles to achieve a murmuration are: creativity, communication, collaboration, change and care.

Principle 1: Creativity

Einstein said that creativity was a key trait of genius. Can an organization or individual evolve without being dynamically creative? Riding the elements of change requires adaptability, presence and creativity. In many organizations the ability to have significantly new ideas actioned rests in the hands of a small percentage of people.

Einstein said that creativity was a key trait of genius.

Perpetually evolving dynamic creativity leads to elasticity of thought, mental regeneration, paradigm-shift thinking and a great sense of humour. We were born creative. It's our primal programming, so we only need simple ways to access it and a fertile environment in which it can flourish. Creativity also breeds accelerated learning.

What if there was an easy and dynamic way for people to access this most formidable part of themselves and make that new acumen a habit? What if this small percentage became 30, 40 or 50 per cent? How would that extended capacity affect the organization's ability to evolve in the face of market changes in real time?

To successfully develop such a system two things are essential: the tools and techniques must be holistically effective – that is, applicable and effective everywhere in a person's life; and a person must be able to realize that the learning is already lodged unconsciously in their behavioural operating system so that they can unlock it and make it habit-forming.

I call this "second nature learning".

Principle 2: Communication

What if the majority of people in an organization communicated succinctly and compellingly?

For 20 years I have been asking people in organizations the same question: if there's one thing you could change that could lead to the greatest leap forward for the organization what would it be? Everyone says the same thing: communication.

The conduit for change, the medium by which we influence flexibility and the means to get things done, is communication. In organizations, our ability to communicate is the beating of our wings. It's what makes us universally effective. Presentations, written communications, one-to-ones and coffee chats are the places where our culture perpetuates itself. When people articulate themselves elegantly, compellingly and with flair everything runs smoother. Clarity breeds confidence. You need confidence when moving into the unknown.

Is great communication optional?

Principle 3: Collaboration

What if every member of an organization was individually autonomous and interdependent? Collaboration is cohesion.

Collaboration in this sense is the key to co-creation, connection, community and leadership. Working as a great team is not the same as great teamworking. A great team-worker can interface with any team, on any project regardless of its culture, hierarchy or history. Starlings don't have to like their neighbours to operate effectively with them. The SAS doesn't need to know the people it depends on to get the job done, and most improvisers only get to meet their co-players when they get on stage.

In a rapidly changing world we cannot get locked into our routines. The flexibility of starlings is dependent on achieving dynamic connection. For humans, that means facilitation, common purpose, great listening and moving beyond office politics.

Principle 4: Change

How many people do you know who are great at change? So much of being good at change is about presence and choice. What trains us to be good at change? Twenty years ago people used to do three-day courses to learn how to use Microsoft Word. Remember that? Can you imagine someone today saying, "Sorry I can't come to your event next week – I'm on a three-day Microsoft Word course". That would be ridiculous. In 20 years' time it will seem equally ridiculous to have to learn how to deal with change. It is the Microsoft Word of today.

Being a "starling at change" means being able to:

- Overcome resistance – yours and someone else's.
- Improve-ise – "Improve-isation" is the ability to positively impact any situation, in the moment; it makes us spontaneously effective.
- Cultivate a passionate curiosity about the unfolding possibilities. That's an attitude and a groove.

What if most of your people not only embraced change wholeheartedly but knew how to use their capacity to change rapidly as a competitive advantage?

Principle 5: Care

Is care a system or a mindset? Organizations without care at their heart are devoid of humanity.

All collective evolution comes down to personal responsibility: care for the self and care for the whole. It all starts and ends with care. Most people talk about care as if it's something "nice to have" in the workplace as opposed to the greatest conductor of personal effectiveness and well-being. And what's the alternative? Not caring? Is that really a viable or desirable option? Care is a fundamental derivative of Purpose. When one is Purposeful one cares about the whole. We cannot give ourselves in the service of an eight, nine or ten possibility without that possibility being one whose benefits spread beyond us. Purposeful people care.

The dysfunctions which govern the way people operate are woven into the cultural fabric of many organizations. Everybody knows that meetings take up too much time but nobody does anything about it, which means that the culture itself is dysfunctional. When we see this and do nothing about it we are colluding to sustain life-leaching dysfunctions. Whose life is it that we are leaching?

A murmuration of Purposeful people represents a cultural shift not just in organizational terms but for the world at large. It moves us away from control to empowerment. There are a few rare people and organizations prepared to embrace such a radical notion, although the ones that do will reinvent all notions of what it means to work.

We are at a tipping point. Rigid control structures are slowing us down; meanwhile, the outside world is galloping apace. Break or flex? Suffer or surf? Nature is our greatest teacher. Murmurations are beautiful, dynamic and highly effective. They are a window into the possibility of Purposeful people working together for the greater good.

Evolution is out of control. Murmurate.

Change is inevitable.
Purpose is the constant.
It is the focus that provides the compass bearing through the fog.
Like a plane we may spend 99 per cent of our time "off target".
Retaining our Purpose keeps us true.

Time

"Time is the most precious commodity I have.
It is the only thing I cannot buy."

Warren Buffett

Remember that 41–50 per cent of our lives preparing for, travelling to and from, or at work? How much value do we give to our time? How much value do we give to our life?

There's an ancient story about a king who wanted to see his land. It had been many years since he rode the boundaries of his kingdom and made contact with his people so he gathered his royal guard and rode out in a white chariot inlaid with gold and pulled by four magnificent white stallions bred from a long line of champion horses.

For months he rode the land, meeting the people. One day he was caught out on the open road in a thunderstorm and it was not long before the wheels became stuck fast in mud. The horses strained but they could not free the chariot from the mud. Eventually the captain of the guard unleashed the horses to rest a while.

Just then an old farmer came up to the scene with two weathered-looking horses and asked the captain if he might try to release the carriage. The captain looked dismissively at the farmer's two horses and asked: "What makes you think you can succeed where these have not?" "Please," replied the farmer.

At that moment the king appeared. He nodded his assent to the captain and the farmer tethered his horses to the carriage. When they were attached the farmer stood between his two faithful steeds. He whispered to them softly, such that only they would hear. He then stepped back, called the command and the two horses as one pushed against the muddy soil. Slowly, the wheels began to move. The farmer called his encouragement, the horses pulled harder and the carriage shifted forward. One final call and the wheels lurched free. All were astonished.

The king called the farmer over to thank him, and gave him some gold for his trouble. He then asked the old man: "What did you say to them? Was it magic?" The farmer smiled and replied: "No sire. I simply reminded them that they are brothers and that if they pull together as one they are far stronger than any four horses who pull as individuals."

Purposeful organizations

When we as individuals are living our Purpose we are no longer fragmented. All parts of ourselves are pulling together to the same ends. The same is true with a team. A group of people who share a common compelling Purpose is unstoppable. This scenario is played out constantly in films... a group of scrappy rebels, outnumbered and under-resourced, fighting against the big machine or state, and yet prevailing through superior grit and ingenuity. Think of *Star Wars* or *The Matrix*, to name just a couple. It is rare to find this quality of common purpose in organizations but when it is cultivated the results are astonishing.

Purposeful organizations have 9 per cent of the human resources costs of non-Purposeful organizations, according to *Authentic Business* by Neil Crofts. Why?

- When people are deeply committed to their organization or team they tend to take fewer arbitrary sick days.
- It is easier to recruit and retain talent.
- Talent becomes more talented as the challenges encourage greater resourcefulness.

- People are more resourceful and take more time and effort to develop themselves.
- They are both fiercely independent and collaborate whole-heartedly.
- They do not waste time or money.
- They focus on being effective rather than being correct or "looking good".

I could go on.

Many years ago I did some work with Peace One Day, founded by the wonderful Jeremy Gilley (www.peaceoneday.org). To give you some history, Jeremy discovered that there has not been a single day of ceasefire in the history of humanity... not one day in recorded history when one group has not been at war with another. He was shocked by this and said to himself that we should have one day – just one – where nobody goes to war with anyone else: "One day of peace... Peace One Day." He had left school at 16 with two O levels, one in drama and the other in metalwork. He had no resources, no money, contacts or organization – just an idea. He started working out of his old bedroom in his mother's house and for two years he contacted everyone of influence he could think of: politicians, actors, business people, spiritual leaders, sports people, the UN... everybody. Six days before the 11 September attacks the United Nations unanimously declared 21 September every year to be the International Day of Peace. On that day there are concerts, pledges of peace from people young and old, ceasefire agreements are drawn up and there is a cessation of hostilities around the world.

When I met Jeremy he had a handful of people working out of borrowed offices in East London. There was barely enough money to pay people for their food. The person with children got the most money regardless of their role. Purpose, passion and commitment brought them greater and greater exposure and success alongside Jeremy's extraordinary powers as a communicator. Now the day is celebrated by hundreds of millions of people around the world and it is here to stay.

I have worked with some of the world's biggest businesses – Google, Coca-Cola, Unilever, Procter & Gamble, Allianz – and even though those organizations are extraordinary and have immensely talented people, I have never seen them emulate the commitment and effectiveness of Peace One Day. Is it the people? I don't think so. It's the Purpose.

Evolving the essence of effectiveness

"Every process of evolution whether technical or biological is about achieving equal or better results with less effort."

If no one reads our lengthy emails at work we change our style. The Purpose becomes more important than our habits. Purposeful people are more effective, not only because the different parts of themselves pull together but because they drop extraneous action. In most organizations more time is spent off Purpose than on it; more time wasted than productive. I once had a conversation with an extremely sophisticated head of IT. I asked him why, when using my Mac, I can get more done with fewer clicks than on a PC. He said: "It's not that you can do more things with an Apple, it's that they know what to leave out – a direct embodiment of Steve Jobs' fascination with Zen." It's the same with Purposeful people. They simply do not spend the time writing a 40-slide presentation when just a handful of slides serve the Purpose more effectively. Simply asking oneself "What is the Purpose of this project?" and "How much does this task serve the Purpose out of ten?" is a revolution in thinking for most people.

Asking "What's the Purpose of this?", seeking the highest possibility and naming the Purpose in less than 15 words gets you to the essence, keeps you to the essence, ensures you dissolve unproductive effort, stops you dissipating your energy, keeps you motivated and makes you grow.

If you are Purposeful in your work you value your time. It's important.

Winning time

So, if we want to win back time, where is it that we lose time?

Everywhere. As Gandhi famously said: "There is more to life than increasing its speed." It's not that we're doing things slowly and that they need to be faster, it is more about not doing the things that waste our time – such as having our horses pulling in different directions or where our lives feel out of control and overtaken by events. It is always about being centred in everything that we do so that we can use our best judgement, focus on the essence and complete tasks well.

There are macro-gains and micro-gains. A meeting, as we will see later, is a macro-gain. It accounts for a huge amount of time at work and we can save 30–50 per cent of it with improved results. Many meetings involve presentations; how long have those taken to create? How much of that time is wasted? How much time could be won back purely by focusing on Purpose and essence? How about applying the same approach to documents, emails, peripheral conversations, internal politics? Each of these areas represents a loss of time, but it's not so much about the time as it is about the loss of energy and the sporadic nature of people's existence, as if the world is happening to us. When we take control of our time, we take control of our lives. When we focus ourselves around Purpose and essence, we focus on meaning. It's so much more satisfying and it's so much simpler. If you had ten books to read and there was an 11th book that would allow you to read the other ten in a fraction of the time you would want to read the 11th book first, wouldn't you? Purpose and essence is that 11th book.

I do an experiment with people on my presentation skills course. I invite them to structure their presentation around questions and simple bullet points. Then I ask them to deliver their structure at the front of the room. I ask them not to embellish or augment in any way and to say it in as few words as possible. To give you an idea, a 20-minute presentation given this way takes under three minutes to speak out. We then find out what people in the audience have remembered from the talk, how much information they have just from the structure and how much more detail they would really need to be able to make decisions related to each topic.

It is remarkable how much we can communicate in a few minutes and how little we really need to make informed decisions. It takes people about 15 minutes to structure a presentation using this method (www.yesindeed.com – look at online courses). It takes a further 30 to develop their stories, data and examples to flesh out their points and a bit more if they want to use visuals. The whole process is designed around Purposeful presentation and getting to the essence. People can create a paradigm-shifting talk at the highest level in under an hour if they wish. They say that it usually takes three–four hours to develop an excellent 20-minute talk. That's a 75 per cent saving. Is it just about saving time, though? How does taking less time affect their results?

There is a law of diminishing return when it comes to communication. An hour-long presentation is not twice as effective as a half-hour-long presentation. Usually the opposite is true. When people can say things more succinctly they are more impactful. It also gives them clarity and, as we've seen, clarity breeds confidence. They learn to trust their intelligence more and the extra time they gain can be used for telling stories and cherry-picking examples to make their point. It's much simpler. The proof, however, in business terms is "How much money did this make us?" Obviously measures of effectiveness are much broader than this, but these techniques have helped my clients close over £2 billion worth of new business in under three years. So it works. Gratifying though that is, the great gain for me is when people come back and tell me how they have been using those same techniques at home and with their children and how much of a difference it makes.

These techniques have been successfully applied to construction, deep science, social issues, environmental concerns, relationships and the plight of refugees, always achieving remarkable results in a short period of time.

There is no relationship between effort and effectiveness. This book is not about giving answers, it's about asking questions and suggesting experiments to help you google your subconscious mind and access your innate genius. The techniques referred to above do the same. *You* are the real genius. The techniques simply help you to access that.

Don't wait ten years to access your genius. Do it now. You'll love it, the people around you will love it and the world will shine brighter as a result.

Your time, your life, life itself is important.
If time is money…
Purposeful time is well spent.

Meetings

I have been having the following conversation with middle management and above in organizations, corporations, not-for-profits and government institutions for over 20 years. The results are always the same, regardless of the nationality, social mix, hair colour or whatever.

Me: "On average, what percentage of your time would you say you spend in meetings?"

Standard response: "...60–70 per cent."

Me: "Blimey! OK... What percentage of that time would you say is eight, nine or ten out of ten useful? Ten out of ten means 'that meeting was fantastic, I loved it, it brought me everything I wanted and more, let's have more like that, rock and roll' and one means 'I just about have a pulse'."

Standard response: "...5–15 per cent of our meetings are eight, nine or ten out of ten effective."

Me: "So, let me get this straight... you're saying that, at most, 15 per cent of 70 per cent of your work life is effective? Are you saying then that up to 50 per cent of our work life is unproductive, irrelevant and, without wanting to labour the point too much, a total waste of time?"

Standard response: *Guilty smiles, feet shuffling, sideways glances to see who agrees and a growing acknowledgement that the person who leads most of their meetings is probably in the room.*

Me: "How much does that cost? Poorly run meetings must be the greatest hidden haemorrhage of cash in any organization. More than the cost of the premises, insurances or most of the salaries. Not to mention the personal cost. I mean, how does it feel to come out of a poorly run two-hour meeting?"

Standard responses: "Drained." "Tiring." "Soul destroying." "I need a triple espresso to start to feel human again."

Me: "So then, why does this happen?"

Standard response: *Silence*.

Me: "We all know that this is the case. Every organization tends to be the same, so why does it carry on? If we know about it, why don't we do something about it?"

Standard response: *Tumbleweeds...*

So why does it carry on happening? I think the answer to this question lies with chimpanzees.

There was an extraordinary experiment done by scientists studying the behaviour of chimpanzees. Five chimps were put in a room. In the centre was a stepladder with a bunch of bananas on the top and water sprinklers were placed in the ceiling. Whenever one of the chimps headed up the ladder to get a banana, the sprinklers came on, dousing them all with cold water. They pretty quickly worked out the relationship between making a move on the bananas and getting soaked, so the moment one of them leapt forth the others pounced on him and beat him up, thus discouraging any more "ladderial" escapades. (Before you ask, I made up the word "ladderial".) After a while no chimps went up the ladder. A norm had been established.

The scientists then turned the sprinklers off, took one of the chimpanzees out of the room and put a fresh one in. Predictably, the new chimp saw the bananas, thought "lunch" and started to scamper up the ladder. The others, equally predictably, grabbed him and beat him up, even though now the sprinklers had not come on. The new chimp obviously had no idea why he or she was being beaten up.

One by one the scientists removed the remaining four from the original group of chimps. Now the room was full of chimps who had never been soaked. What happens when one of them decides to go for the bananas? Yep... they get beaten up. Why? Because "that's the way things are done around here" – a new cultural norm has been established. A culture that endures beyond the initiating generation.

What is so important about this is that it reveals behaviours have been set as patterns for the micro-society. They need no foundation of reason and no effort to perpetuate. A new norm is established and the chimps abide by the self-imposed rules until a newer social norm is established. It is quick to establish and hard to eradicate.

But we're people not chimps, we're much more sophisticated than that; I mean, "think how far we've come since the invention of navel-gazing" I hear you cry. OK, let's have a look at the human animal...

Some 100,000–150,000 years ago there were two species of humanity... Cro-Magnon and the new kid on the block, *Homo sapiens*. Although they had similar sized and shaped brains, Cro-Magnon was the stronger of the two, and a better hunter with keener senses. *Homo sapiens* was slighter, less physically capable but was a more effective social animal. Which of these two would you assume is most likely to survive in a sabre-toothed world?

The winner is, of course, *Homo sapiens*, who created more sophisticated social structures and was therefore able to leverage collective intelligence more effectively. *Homo sapiens* worked better together. We are *Homo sapiens*. If we could take a child from 100,000 years ago and bring them up in today's world, they would be able to use iPads, ride bicycles and argue about bedtimes.

It is said that 60 per cent of our *Homo sapiens* DNA is devoted to collective consciousness – 60 per cent! What does this really mean for us? It means that we are programmed to fit in, to observe and position ourselves with regard to the established norm... a bit like walking into a party where we don't know anybody, taking refuge next to a wall, grabbing a drink as cover and seeing how the land lies, sensing the social norms before deciding whether to delight the room with our best moves. This positioning can make us contravene or sustain the status quo but there is an instinctive awareness and relationship to it nonetheless.

So what's all this got to do with meetings? I think this is what happens when we join a new organization – mixed obviously with a smidgen of ironic irreverence just to keep it interesting: We start off bright eyed and bushy tailed, keen to make a good impression, turn up to our first meeting, iPhone turned off, notebook out, brand new shiny pen poised and ready to take down action points and pearls of organizational wisdom and then... we start to do the "going-to-a-party-where-we-don't-know-anybody" routine. That is, we pay attention to what's going on to discover the social norms. It can look something like this: "*Should I speak? I'll wait a bit. Ooh, I've got an idea... Oh, it seems like there's not much room to speak here. Hmmm, what's the dialogue between those two?... No space for the rest of us to get involved... How come this guy keeps on going on... and on... and on? Why doesn't somebody say something? ... Oh, OK... so we're supposed to sit here and... listen... and listen more... that's the way things are done around here, is it? Right, make a note: 'Meetings are not really meetings they're "long listenings".' Got it.*" A year on and... does that person even question the meetings culture any more? They have just accepted that when they get around a table at work they are entering a half-life, a twilight zone of semi-reality.

Maybe that's a bit harsh, but for more than two decades every organization I have ever been in says that's pretty much exactly what goes on. It turns out that the people who say that up to 50 per cent of their meetings are highly effective are actually the people who are running the meetings. Hmmmm.

Why do we maintain the spirit-withering practice that typifies practically ALL meetings? The answer to this question is: That's the way things are done around here. It's our culture and we are so used to it, so inured, that we do not realize it's going on any more. I mean, does a fish know that it's in water?

If face-to-face meetings have this purgatorial feel, what of virtual meetings? A client of mine who is a vice president of a Fortune 50 corporation says, "I love virtual meetings. It's the only chance I have to do my emails." For most people the virtual meeting routine goes... *Dial-in, say hello, press mute, do something else.* Attention spans are shorter, there's no body language to speak of and thus no subliminal signals, tonality and vocal nuance afford little subtlety and we are forever backtracking and apologizing for speaking at the same time as someone else. The net result is that virtual meetings become voice-overed PowerPoint presentations. How would you describe most of the PowerPoint presentations you sit through when you are in the same room as the speaker? Would you want to watch them on television when you got home from work? Exactly. That's what virtual meetings are like for most people.

When did we decide that it was OK to spend vast tranches of our lives bored out of our minds?

It's not all doom and gloom, though. Somebody once said: "You don't have to die to go to Heaven. You just have to stop going to Hell." A shift of focus in meetings, a few key behaviours and a radical rethinking of our agendas is all it takes to turn the 60 longest minutes of your life into vibrant debate and decision-making crafted into bite-sized chunks.

Unsurprisingly, this process of transformation starts with Purpose:

What's the Purpose of the meeting? In less than 15 words, this Purpose needs to be articulated in terms of the outcome the meeting is designed to generate... What happens as a result of this meeting having achieved its Purpose at an eight, nine or ten out of ten? This focuses people, changes the way they show up, drives our intent toward the outcome and lobotomizes a whole host of issues.

Who needs to be there to serve this Purpose at an eight, nine or ten out of ten? Have you ever watched a film you don't know in a language you don't understand? That's what it's like sitting through a meeting that has no relevance for you. Addressing this question frees up people's time, ensures that those gathered have something tangible to offer and keeps the trajectory of a project relevant.

We then go on to create an agenda based on questions rather than headings and establish a set of behaviours that is inclusive, creative and where the chairperson operates as a conduit for the collective intelligence of the room. A full working explanation of the system would be (and probably will be) a separate book. However, you can find out more at www.yesindeed.com (look at online courses). It's a radical approach to running Purposeful meetings. It saves people 30–50 per cent of the time they spend in meetings with better quantifiable outputs.

Meetings are the principal artery of organizational practice.
They can make or break any project.
Work can be a thrilling co-creative ride or it can be life-leaching.
What's the Purpose of this meeting?
Who serves the Purpose eight, nine or ten out of ten?
That's where it begins...

Politics

I studied Politics as an undergraduate. Ironically, it prepared me extremely well for working with large organizations.

I remember walking into a lecture on my first day at university. The professor asked whether anyone knew what the word "politics" means? I had absolutely no idea. A few people called out hopeful suggestions, such as "change", "governance", "leadership".

"No," said the professor, "it means power-play."

I remember sinking in my seat. I was not interested in power-play. I was interested in change and progress. These things seemed to have nothing to do with power-play. As I studied the political landscape more intensively and watched the nightly posturing on the news, I knew that he was right. The overwhelming majority of people involved in politics are engaged in power-play for their own ends and not for the sake of the whole. Can that ever be an eight, nine or ten?

Nearly every organization I have worked with has been political. Not in a party-political way but in terms of office politics. It's a massive waste of time and is ALWAYS a distraction from what needs to be done – a powerful horse pulling in a different direction.

The more that people identify with their work, the more they need to "look good" to satisfy their self-esteem and the more they politic. Purpose is about serving something bigger than ourselves for the benefit of the highest good. Politics is about serving oneself, often in spite of the highest good. When the two are placed side by side, Purpose always wins. Politics doesn't know how to deal with it.

Purpose and values' statement

I was once asked by a major international architectural practice to develop an appraisal system, a series of questions to help run effective appraisals and enhance the connection and rapport between managers and their teams. I asked what their Purpose and values were. The puzzled and slightly overwhelmed HR person asked: "Why, what difference does that make?"

I said: "If your people are focused on the Purpose of the organization and can have an authentic, beneficial conversation in line with the values, you almost don't need a piece of paper with lots of questions on it. If, however, they can't have an authentic conversation, it doesn't really matter what's on the piece of paper, they will find a way around it. It makes sense then to work out what your Purpose and values are first and then design everything else to serve them."

So that's what we did. I led a meeting with the heads of department and directors to determine the Purpose and values. It was extremely bizarre. From the very beginning of the meeting people were aggressive. Everybody disagreed with everybody else and it all came through me. I was at the front of the room busy tai chi-ing one snipe after another. I suddenly realized that these people didn't even know me, so it couldn't be personal. There must be something going on in the group. Then I noticed that one person was causing all the ruckus. Every wave of dissent started or ended with him. I began to ask different kinds of questions and we moved closer and closer to realizing a Purpose statement for the business. At that point this man started to shout at me. He quoted phrases attributed to the Sanhedrin and the Pharisees in the New Testament, and when these attacks did not have the desired effect he started to insult me personally. I told him that I was here to serve the group and his business but that I warmly did not care if I ever worked with them again, my children would eat regardless and I wasn't going to change my views because someone was screaming and shouting. The loudest voice often wins but it rarely works in favour of the highest good. My role was to uphold the eight, nine or ten possibility for the organization and to help it become a reality. It was impersonal. At that point, he stood up, threw a final insult in my direction and stormed out of the room. Within 90 seconds of him leaving we arrived at the Purpose statement for the organization, which they still adhere to today.

I realized two things after the event:

1. Nobody at that level in the organization had authentic conversations with each other, which was the reason for the dissent. Everything therefore had to come through the facilitator because they were incapable of speaking to each other.
2. As we began to arrive at a common compelling Purpose the atmosphere became intolerable for the director, who thrived on internal politics. His power base sprang from sowing dissent... divide and conquer. Common Purpose was therefore an element in which he could not play. The moment people could have authentic conversations and champion something greater than themselves, his game was up. He felt it and left the room. He left the company within a month and the others thrived as a result.

Systems theorist Buckminster Fuller said: "You can never change things by fighting. You have to create something new which makes the existing reality obsolete." Purpose and politics don't mix. One serves the whole. The other serves itself.

Purpose and politics

I had a similar situation occur when I was asked to run a common Purpose session for the Abrahamic faiths – Jews, Christians and Muslims. It was a gorgeous and irresistible possibility. If these three faiths, which have been at loggerheads with each other for hundreds of years, had a common Purpose what would it be? If they could live it, what would change in the world? Would people embrace a Purpose that united them with others who prayed differently?

The session ran beautifully right up until we started to formulate the Purpose statement. One woman in the group then spontaneously began to disrupt proceedings. None of her objections were sustainable and each one looked and felt like a clumsy attempt to draw attention away from where we were heading and engage the group in divisive conversations. It was almost a cut-and-paste of the encounter with the architects but with a Christian gentleness. The group, although amenable to discussing her issues, was focused on achieving the outcome. She could not divide the group and felt compelled to leave, citing an issue with health that seemed to spring up from nowhere. Within minutes we had found a Purpose statement that resonated deeply throughout the group and which, if applied, could trigger deep reverberations across the faiths. The Purpose statement read: "The Abrahamic faiths serve the Purpose of Generating Spiritual Values." When we explored this in more detail it became clear that each of the faiths seemed to share the same values and that by living them, comparing them and sharing stories about them their penetrating beauty became obvious to all. They were – are, in fact – perfectly harmonious and, at best, a variation on a theme of each other. Like separate musical notes which, when played together, form a harmony.

Some people define themselves by being against things... Something has to be "bad" for what they want to be "good". It seems a very unhappy way to run one's life to me. The woman who left the room somehow felt her faith and identity were being threatened by embracing and appreciating other forms of expression to the one she had allied herself to. She could not abide this "attack" on her carefully protected mindset and left. Is French cooking any less delicious if one also appreciates Italian, Indian or Chinese food? Surely the appreciation of other forms of cuisine makes one a better cook? Appreciating the different ways in which Jews, Christians and Muslims explore and express core human values must make us more Value-able.

Purpose is the antidote to politics.

Politics divides. Purpose unites.

When one returns to the Purpose of a project, an initiative or a plan, divisive conversations tend to evaporate.

The following six behaviours have been identified over the years as typical of an office politician:

- They block suggestions around everything except the outcome they are looking to achieve. "Yes but..." and "The problem is..." are favourite expressions.
- Being non-committal around projects and outcomes until decision time – and then they attack it in prominent moments... such as at a key meeting, after a presentation and so on.
- Working the corridors – having little, informal conversations during which they sow seeds of doubt about other people, mostly in a seemingly reasonable and kind way but always focused on negating someone else's influence. "He/she has excellent qualities but I think they would thrive more in this

area rather than that one." "She seems tired recently; it would be unwise to give her more responsibility so soon."

- Insisting on putting their name to projects which are becoming prominent or successful. There's a "final rush" to take credit – "I will present it with our results at the executive meeting"... "I will include it in my briefing, there is no need for both of us to be there."
- CC'ing people higher up in the organization in emails as a way of putting pressure on peers.
- Masking criticism with concern. Instead of openly criticizing others with whom they feel competitive, they tend to shift people's focus onto "concerns"... "I'm concerned that she has too much on at the moment, or is being pulled in too many directions"... "It may be good to park that for a while, I'm not sure his team could handle it"... "This may prove too much of a distraction from their core work, it might be better if we retain this function for the time being."

There are two excellent ways of handling the office politician:
1. Listen very carefully (actually this is always a solution to issues) while holding a focus on the Purpose of a project.
2. Re-centre every conversation around that Purpose.

Office politician: "I'm not sure that this project is right for 'x' to lead, it may prove too much for them."

You, *clarifying the person's position without having any point of view*: "Are you suggesting moving it to someone else or cancelling it altogether?"

Office politician: "I think we should shift responsibility for the project to another two people in my department. I would be happy to supervise them."

You: "I see. So we are agreed that the project serves the highest good but you're concerned about 'x' leading it?"
Office politician, *nodding*.
You: "The Purpose of this project is... the question then is 'who is the best person to achieve it?' If I think about it 'x' has all the qualities and experience to run the project and the advantages for the organization are this, this and this. It really would be a perfect outcome if we could help them achieve it. So, then, how do we help them become successful?"

Now you are in a conversation about supporting "x" in achieving their goals because the focus is achieving the greatest outcomes for the organization (the Purpose). It becomes very hard for the office politician to steer things against this tide. If they do, just refocus them on the Purpose.

Sponsoring questions

"The question is..." is a perfect statement. It allows you to refocus any conversation, either one-to-one or in a meeting, toward the Purpose.

- "The question is... how do we achieve 'x' (the Purpose)?"
- "The question is... how can we help 'x' achieve 'y'?"
- "The question is... who is the best team to get us there?" And so on.

President John F Kennedy used sponsoring questions time and time again. The wonderful film *13 Days* (http://www.imdb.com/title/tt0146309/) follows the president during the Cuban Missile Crisis and many of the conversations were taken from transcripts of meetings in the Oval Office during that time. Kennedy focuses the Purpose of the conversation using "the question is..." and does not commit to one perspective over another until all the facts are known. The forces around him try incessantly to push him into war but he refuses. "The question is..." and a focus on Purpose may be the reason why we did not have a nuclear war in 1962.

For 25 years I have been running change programmes in highly politicized atmospheres. More so now than ever before. In that time my brief is always to trigger a sustainable mindset and behavioural shift in people ranging from the heads of the organization to the front line. I have to get people to do things without me having any position in the hierarchy. I can't just say "do this please", my only route is influence. Because I tend to speak to people at every level of the organization, and often have more exposure to the CEO than most others, people often see me as a "political vehicle". This means that they say things to me in the hope that I will pass messages, make comments or influence outcomes in ways favourable to them – they try to use me to further their political ends. The Purpose of politics is personal advancement. The Purpose of Purpose is collective benefit. Maintaining my focus on the Purpose of a project or moment has proven frictionless time and time again. It gets the job done and it leaves no scars. When we maintain our focus on Purpose we don't get distracted; our path stays true. Politicians try to manipulate. Purposeful people try to elevate. When you stick to the Purpose you become UNMANIPULATABLE.

Experiments

Listen carefully and sum people up cleanly in one sentence or bullet point.

So the Purpose is...

So the question is... (watch *13 Days*).

Keep on asking yourself "What's the Purpose here?" and you will be UNMANIPULATABLE.

If you resonate with this approach have a look at "Articulate Listening" (www.yesindeed.com – look at online courses).

4

Purpose in Action

I am aware as I write this that I am as much a student of this book as I am its author. I practise everything I write, and where I do not I eventually discover that if I practise more of what I write every gap would be bridged.

The focus of this section is to turn the positive intent and possibility that our Purpose represents into actions and results which transform our lives and touch others. My aim here is to pass on the essence of everything I have learned in the application of Purpose in my own experience and through the experiences of the 200,000 or so people I have facilitated. In 25 years I have experimented with so many different techniques, approaches and philosophies. The ones I share here are the ones I know to be extremely resilient, flow with the approach we have already adopted and have proved to be both successful and fun for the greatest number.

When people look to action their Purpose, key distinctions and questions tend to come up – these are addressed in Fundamentals at the beginning of this part of the book. Next, in order to make Purposeful goals you will need to have a simple, creative method, which is set out here in Honeycombs. The successful manifestation of those goals is the result of putting into action the six principles of Purpose, which are:

- Be Absolute.
- Be Persistent.
- Be Positive.
- Be in Action.
- Be Game.
- Clear the Past.

Each of these principles is explored, accompanied by a variety of experiments that will keep things interesting. Although there are more than six experiments, each is a simple expression of the principles. Ideally, you will try the experiments that appeal to you most so that you can integrate the principle and then adapt the tools and techniques, making them your own. Please then share your experiments on the Facebook page for the book so that we all grow (Facebook: The 7 Questions to Find Your Purpose).

Fundamentals

Sometimes when people are at the outset of a new phase, stage or venture there are some common issues which rear their heads. In the following section are some of the most commonly occurring ones, along with tried and tested ways of dealing with them.

80:20

Remember the iceberg model? It revealed that 80 per cent of our mind is the unconscious and 20 per cent the conscious. Our power of manifestation lies in the alignment of these two. Imagine for a moment that your mind was an airplane. The conscious mind would be the joystick or control wheel, the rudder pedals and the radio. Mastering these is essential to pilot the plane – however, it's not the whole story. You also need to be able to read the instruments... radar, altimeter, compass, airspeed indicator, heading indicator and so on. These instruments are the unconscious mind. You simply can't get to where you want to go easily without everything working together.

As you read the suggestions and experiments in the following pages you might wonder why we are doing a particular exercise. It's nearly always a way of engaging or aligning the conscious and unconscious.

True discipline

Most people think that to get where they want to go they need discipline. When I ask them what they mean by discipline they give me an image of gritted teeth, straining tendons, perspiration and US Navy

Sealdom, force and effort, usually in spite of what they find pleasurable, and accompanied by a heavy dose of self-sacrifice. That, undoubtedly, is many people's view of what brings results. It's certainly one that's popularized in the films that have replaced mythology in our society. Is that it? Is that the real meaning of "discipline"? Is that what you need to do to live your Purpose in life and feel in your last breath that you've achieved something?

I have two cats. I'm always amazed at how they can lie around the house for days on end, stretched out, curled up and behaving more like warm, fluffy cushions than creatures at the head of the food chain. And yet, the moment their instincts are called upon they are capable of the most extraordinary feats of athleticism. Their abilities are innate – and what's more, they seem to revel and thrive in them. We too have instincts and senses, which are as finely tuned as those of cats. If we use our intuitive senses as much as we do our eyes and ears, we will experience the timeless, invincible part of ourselves.

The word "discipline" derives from "disciple", which literally means "joyful follower". A far cry from the sweaty, straining popular vernacular. "Joyful follower." Let's remember that our Purpose is what truly says "YES" to us on a core level of eight, nine or ten out of ten. If that does not invoke joy, and therefore joyful following, what does?

In 25 years of exploration in shamanism, business effectiveness, competitive sport, yoga, the healing arts, mediation in a myriad of forms and hard work, the most effective and enjoyable way I have discovered of releasing our capacities and creating the life we most want to live is through play, experimentation and joyful interaction. So those are the areas I have explored the most and therefore the ones I can pass on most faithfully. Some of these methods of pursuing our Purpose may be unusual but they are always stretching and experimental. Our Purpose is bigger than us – that is why it is something we serve rather than something we are. The only frictionless path to living it, which engages all of ourselves therefore, is exploration. Play for me is a massively underrated area of personal development and self-realization. When play applies to Purpose it inevitably leads to "joyful following" and thus, true discipline.

Make or break?

One of the questions that often comes up for people as they consider the reality of manifesting their Purpose is: "Do I have to change everything now that I have my Purpose?" Usually they mean, do I have to change my job/partner/where I live?

The answer is "of course not"… and "of course". Of course you do not have to do anything that you don't want to do and of course you will inevitably want to make changes.

You have an opportunity to create what says "YES" to you at an eight, nine or ten out of ten. That's it. Usually this means making refinements and improvements to all areas of your life incrementally. We make it up as we go. Occasionally, we have a "bolt from the blue" – a piece of inspiration so significant that we have to just jump. Much of the time when this happens the other parts of our life were so out of alignment with what says "YES" to us most that we really didn't lose anything by making the leap. Einstein was a clerk in a patent office. He did his research in his spare time and was always frustrated with the fact that he was not playing on a bigger stage, working full-time on proving his theories. His wife got so sick and tired of hearing the same story that she eventually left him. His life hit a point of impasse, so he jumped into the life that said "YES" to him most. He changed the shape of global thinking as a result. That leap may have felt huge at the time, but the reality was that he had nothing to lose. JK Rowling beautifully describes that moment when "rock bottom became the solid foundation on which I rebuilt my life". In the vast majority of cases we can grow our relationships instead of changing partners, improve our job not jack it in, see some friends more and others less. Reiterating the earlier Buckminster Fuller quote, we "create something new which makes the existing reality obsolete". Or as Erkhart Tolle beautifully put it: "Nothing of any real value can be lost in the presence of a greater truth."

There is one thing that will have to go if you are to live your Purpose, and that is the fantasy of your life. You cannot live it without allowing the fantasy to become a reality.

This is harder than it seems for some people. Fantasies are safe. We know how to generate them. We know how they can satisfy, up to a point, and we never fail. They also never come to fruition unless we are willing to move them into a place of action and realization. That's the adventure.

I remember coaching someone using Purpose as our foundation. He had a wonderful imagination and when it came to imagining the possibility of living his Purpose, the images and the ideas flowed. When it came to actioning those ideas, progress was extremely slow. He could achieve so much in other parts of his life that I wondered what it was that impeded him in the area that was so obviously his eight, nine, ten. As we talked and I asked him questions, I watched him very closely. Neuro-linguistic programming (NLP) speaks a lot about how the eyes operate in the same way as a mouse for a computer, accessing different parts of the mind. When he spoke about the challenges and opportunities he faced in his daily life, his work plans and the way they were unfolding, his eyes would always flick to the same place as if accessing a particular part of his brain. When he recounted his visions of living his Purpose, he would inevitably look in a different place. I asked him about dreams he had had and about films he had seen. He "clicked" in the same place as his fantasies. When I asked him about his home, his holidays or his son, his eyes "clicked" on the place where he stored his day-to-day matters. Toward the end of the session I asked him to take all his visions of Purpose, to lift them out of their cupboard in his mind, and carry them over to the wardrobe of his day-to-day. He immediately became extremely uncomfortable – fidgeting, looking at his watch, trying to avoid eye contact. I stayed with it and gently asked him to move things one piece at a time – as if moving house. Eventually, he settled and was able to transfer things from one cupboard to another. When I asked him about his Purpose visions again, his eyes "clicked" on the day-to-day place. When they didn't, we moved more stuff. Eventually he had moved house.

Less than a month later, he started his own business. As the saying goes...

"A ship in the harbour is safe, but that's not what ships are built for."

John A. Shedd

Honeycombs

One night my wife and I were walking along the beach in the Caribbean and we saw a huge female turtle laying her eggs in the sand. A few nights later a separate batch of eggs was hatching. These tiny creatures were digging through the sand and making a fearless 100-metre dash toward the sea. With so many creatures waiting for them on the sand, in the air and in the surf this was a particularly intense rite of passage.

I got chatting to a conservation specialist who was observing the hatching. I asked him why, given the precariousness of the little turtles' initiation, they did not simply put them in a bucket, take them out to sea and bypass all the dangers. He said: "We used to do that, but then we found out that the turtles couldn't find their way back to the beach when they wanted to give birth."

"Really?" I asked. "How come?"

"When the baby turtle breaks through the sand," he explained, "it makes its way toward the greatest light source. In a natural surrounding, that is the horizon. If they survive, the only time they will come back to that beach is when the females lay their eggs, which is approximately 30 years after they hatch. They may have swum all around the world in that time but they always come back to the exact same beach where they were born to lay their eggs."

"How do they find their way back?"

"There is a tiny crystal in their brains. When they make their first journey from the egg to the ocean, this crystal is magnetically charged with the exact longitude and latitude reference of the place. It's their homing beacon and they always find their way back."

Imagine for a moment that our Purpose is that "crystal" inside us. When we name it in truth, the "crystal" is fused with our intuition in much the same way as the turtle's. We have our own built-in radar to seek out everything and everyone who helps us live our Purpose to the full. The honeycomb process is a way of setting goals, through harnessing our creative intuition, which express our Purpose eight, nine or ten out of ten.

A ten-step path

The logical paths to goal-setting require hard work and dedication. The intuitive, ten-step path asks you to do two things – to trust and to listen. You'll need your notepad and pencil for this bit.

1. Draw a hexagon in the middle of a clean page with the extra lines (as illustrated). Write your Purpose statement in the middle.

   The actor Matthew McConaughey tells a lovely story of being asked when he was a kid "who's your hero?" and not being able to find an answer. He thought about this question for a long time and eventually came back to his teacher and said, "My hero is me in ten years' time." He holds an image of himself as he would most like to be in ten years' time. He invests his hero-self with his eight, nine or ten choices and constantly emulates the image, literally becoming the hero. It works for him. It is a choice he makes every day. That is the true nature of choice. His evolution from a matinee idol to an actor with depth and gravitas is remarkable.

   If you like the sound of this exercise, write out a description of your "hero-self" and then sum it up in a few words or a picture and place that in the centre of your hexagon.

2. Write a list of six major areas of your life. These might include relationship, family, career, health, spirituality, fun, personal development, finance, social, travel or other personal ambitions.

3. Put down the names of the areas that you feel most accurately reflect the major areas in your life. It's important that you look at what really matters here. It helps to limit these categories to one-word titles. Your hexagon might be starting to look like this:

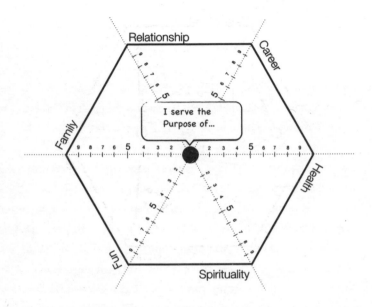

4. Have a look at your hexagon. How complete does it feel to you out of ten as a representation of the key areas of your life? If it is below a nine out of ten, what would you have to do to pop it up?

You will notice on the diagram that each of the lines leading from the centre of the hexagon to its edge is numbered from one to ten. Counting the outside edge as the ten and the centre as zero, and looking at one area of your life at a time, answer the following:

5. If you were to know how much you were living your Purpose out of ten in this area, you'd probably say... out of ten?

Mark that number down on the corresponding line.

Move through each area asking the same question.

When you have finished, join the dots.

Your hexagon might look something like this:

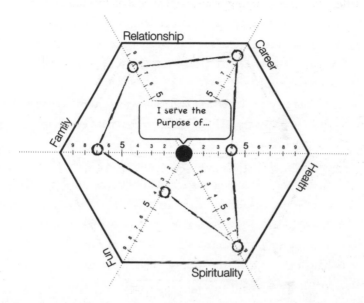

Balance is a key to harmonious living and the hexagon is a naturally balanced shape. Looking at your diagram it will become obvious which places will give the clearest results if you give them your attention. These are the places to start setting goals.

6. Set your goals.

7. Choose an area of your hexagon. Using your intuition, complete the following:

If in six months' time, you were living your Purpose at an eight, nine or ten out of ten at work/with your family, you would probably be doing things like...

Write down your answers.

How much does your goal say "YES" to you on a core level out of ten? What do you have to do for it to be an eight or above?

8. Further develop goals that express your Purpose in each of these areas.

The more specific and infused with your Purpose your goals are, the greater chance you have of success. Make each goal:

Realistic. Does your intuition think that your goal is realistic? Do you believe it?

Achievable. Are you setting yourself a goal that is achievable or are you trying to pile too much on yourself? For example, aim for balance.

Specific. Be clear about your goal. Generalized goals, such as "Get better at...", lead to generalized results. The more specific you can be, the clearer your results. Give it a time limit. What is the date and time by when you will have completed your goal? For example, "By Monday 17 July at 5pm, I will have..."

Enhancing. Does this move you beyond your present circumstances?

9. Visualize the perfect picture. Imagine that your goal has been completed perfectly. How does that area of your life look? What is going on? Describe the perfect completion of your goal. Make your picture full and vibrant. Enjoy its perfection. See as much detail as you can. If you could smell or sense or taste or listen to the quality of that moment what would be there? What would you have to do to move that image to a ten out of ten? Include your answer to this question in your overall answer.

Looking at the *quality* of your ten-out-of-ten image, what does it remind you of? If it were a scene or a picture what would it be? It would be a bit like...

For example, if you were imagining your perfect relationship, it might be a bit like two blue whales swimming together on the high seas, finding a place to have their baby – nuzzling each other as they move, massaging and caressing each other with their sounds. Or it might be more like strawberries dipped in warm chocolate. You choose. The subconscious mind loves metaphors. Go for it. Create to your heart's content. When you do, the vision becomes tactile and tangible.

10. Draw icons or find an object.

Look at what you've written in step 9, and alongside the words draw an icon or image, inside a circle, which speaks of the quality of your goal. The forming of anything new, including creating your Purpose goals, is a creative process. The more you engage your creative mind at the outset the easier it is for your goals to come to fruition. Make it beautiful. Make it rich. Make it so that when you look at your picture or icon again in two months' time you will be able to connect to its quality and the outcome you desire. You can also choose an object here if you prefer.

Complete these ten steps for each area of your life, or as many as you wish to work on. Set yourself the amount of goals or challenges that feel appropriate to you now. If you set too many you may unbalance yourself and it will seem burdensome. Too few and the changes are slower. My suggestion is to set three goals at a time.

Reward yourself

Most people don't spend a lot of time rewarding or recognizing themselves or others. Of course, appreciation helps us enormously and as a strategy for success it's common sense, but is it common practice?

Reward and acknowledgement are very important parts of any goal-setting process and are essential for a balanced life. Purpose without fun becomes duty and that's more akin to sacrifice. Life is for living; reward and acknowledgement are ways of celebrating that. You can choose to reward yourself weekly, monthly, at the end of goals or at milestones along the way there. Regular reward is a good, nourishing thing. Choose what most suits you.

Jim Carrey tells a story of when he was a young unknown. His dream was to be paid US$1 million for acting. He wrote himself a cheque for that amount and put it in his wallet. For years he carried it around even when it become frayed and tattered. When he did *Dumb and Dumber*, he was paid exactly US$1 million.

Set yourself a juicy reward and write that next to or on your icon.

Sign and date the reward to reinforce the fact that it's going to happen.

Principle One: Be Absolute

STOP BEING CAREFUL. START BEING CRUCIAL.

"Until one is committed, there is hesitancy, the chance to draw
back. Concerning all acts of initiative (and creation), there is one
elementary truth that ignorance of which kills countless ideas and
splendid plans: that the moment one definitely commits oneself,
then Providence moves too. All sorts of things occur to help one
that would never otherwise have occurred. A whole stream of events
issues from the decision, raising in one's favour all manner of
unforeseen incidents and meetings and material assistance, which
no man could have dreamed would have come his way. Whatever
you can do, or dream you can do, begin it.
Boldness has genius, power, and magic in it. Begin it now."

Goethe

Bob Marley used to work his energy up before writing the songs that
have become world anthems. He called it "lively up yourself". For him
this meant running uphill, swimming in the sea, eating fresh healthy
food and then writing. He inevitably had a smoke somewhere in that
too, knowing him; however, he used to raise his energy before engaging
his creative mind.

Sport is an excellent way of engaging with "absolute energy". When
I used to play rugby our coach used to say that if you go into a tackle
80 per cent committed, you'll probably get hurt. If you go in 90 per
cent committed, you'll also probably get hurt. But if you go in 100 per
cent committed you'll go straight through your opponent. Everything
gets much easier when we are committed, and committed means being
absolute.

Absolute energy makes things happen. Of all the lines from the magnificent *Lord of the Rings*, the one that is most often quoted is when Gandalf stands on the stone bridge facing his soul's nemesis, the infinitely more powerful Balrog, and cries defiantly "You shall not pass!" This moment of absolute commitment engages a greater energy than he has ever known, is what helps him defeat his enemy and ultimately leads to his transition to a higher level of being. The fastest and most effective way of manifesting our desires is when we can commit to its reality with the same quality of absolute commitment.

- What do you need to do to find that within yourself?
- How can you "lively up yourself"?
- How can you become so committed that you will do what needs to be done – whatever that may be – and let the chips fall where they may?

Twenty-five years of coaching have revealed some repeated patterns. When people are going through a rut or are in transition and don't trust themselves to make eight, nine or ten decisions for themselves, I often ask them: "Are you fit?"

Client: "Er sort of. What do you mean?"

Me: "What do you do physically? For sport?"

Client: "Not much. Go to the gym occasionally."

Me: "Do you like it?"

Client: "Well... it's convenient. I can go there after work and it keeps the blood circulating."

Me: "How do you feel when you're doing it? Is there anything you enjoy more?"

Client: "It's just convenient. No, I find it pretty boring actually. I put the music on, get it done and come home."

Me: "What would you love to do that also gets you physically fit?"

Client: "Well, I used to love running. Actually, dancing. I love dancing, but I can't do that, can I?"

Me: "Why not?"

Client: "I can't get fit dancing, can I?"

Me: "Would you say that dancers are fit?"

Client: "Amazingly so."

Me: "So...?"

Client: "But how am I going to find somewhere I can dance and...?"

Me: "That's what Google is for."

We both look at our phones.

How often are we settling for fives, sixes and sevens instead of just going for our eights, nines and tens. Put every decision on a scale and action eights and above. That's it. It's so easy.

So the client goes dancing and guess what? Not only do they get fit (as well as clarity of thinking, emotional stability, enhanced breathing and digestion, better sleep, more energy) but they also reconnect with what makes them move at an eight, nine or ten out of ten (reconnecting them with forgotten parts of themselves, rekindling a love of music, meeting new people, making new connections, having fun). It's a win-win-win.

The moment they get fit, they change... everything changes for the better.

Now imagine *doing* your eight, nine or ten out of ten. In other words, go dancing and engage with it eight, nine or ten out of ten. How much does that help you give yourself? How are you going to feel the next day? How much easier is it to give yourself equally to the tasks you perform? What insight does that give you about yourself as an eight, nine or ten being? All experience translates.

When I was at school I played water polo. It's a hardcore sport. It took hours of training just to be match fit. And we gave ourselves to it wholeheartedly. It was as if the whole team spurred each other on, like geese. And the more we did the more we won. And we won everything. It was great.

That experience translated into how I gave myself in acting. I gave everything. I could become another person wholly, and it was because of my experience in the pool that I knew how to engage.

One day, a Sunday actually, I was woken up by friends of mine from Drama School. They rang on my bell to get me to an audition in Covent Garden. It was a dance audition. I did not train as a dancer so I thought my chances were thin to say the least. Coupled with that I was in a show at the time, six nights per week and three matinees. It was full of complicated sword fighting, I was knackered and making the most of my day off. I ended up going to the audition. There were 400 people there and six male parts available. It was one of those auditions where people are tapped on the shoulder and asked to leave. If you didn't get the tap you were still on. I just made it all up. I didn't really know what the choreography was, I had no vocabulary of movements so I approximated what I saw and just had a go. An hour later I had a contract to dance with the Royal Opera. Who knew?

On my first day of rehearsal I had to do a ballet class. Ballet. I had studied martial arts but that's about as far from ballet as football is from badminton. I remember sitting in a corner of the dance studio in my sweat pants waiting for the class to begin. A girl came in, threw her bag into the corner, dropped into a full box splits and started complaining about her hangover. I thought, "I'm finished." How on earth was I going to get through six weeks of this, plus performances, on the biggest stage in the land?

I couldn't have done it without water polo.

All experience translates.

Experiments

Find the workout that says "YES" to you eight, nine or ten out of ten.

Plan and execute actions with the same quality.

Humour

Humour is much underestimated as a way of engaging with the world. Many people associate humour with being frivolous and not taking things sincerely. In reality humour can significantly help people in the realization of their goals.

When I was a teenager I remember seeing something amazing in Desmond Morris's book *Manwatching*. There were two photographs side by side. One of them was of a person crying out in anger and the other was someone laughing hysterically. The caption underneath read "Which one do you think is laughing and which one is crying?" When I looked at the pictures, it was hard to tell the difference. Morris went on to explain that anger and humour are very similar in their states. I was fascinated by that and still am. I have noticed that people can create great catharsis through shared pain. It can motivate them to change in many ways and it makes them aware as all intense experience can. As can humour. Truths are sown deep when we laugh as we take them in, like a sugar cube for a vaccine. When we laugh we instinctively move toward the thing that brings about such mirth. And if there are 50 emails in our in-tray and one of them looks like it's going to be funny, which one do we open first?

Humour can be just as cathartic, motivating and insightful as pain. Same muscle group. It's just more fun. Watching comedians talk about the things we find stressful can be a wonderful way of enlightening the load.

Comedy is extreme sanity.

The motto for happiness in life is "do what you love and love what you do".

Some things I absolutely love doing. Others not so much. If I find a way to love the not so much, it becomes great fun. For example, I was running a series of seminars for a client. I had to create variations on a theme for each department. When it came to the last seminar I thought to myself, "I can't do the same old same old; I have to do something different" – even just for my own sanity. So I invented a new way of running the seminar using theatre, drama and interactive comedy. Great fun, and it has led to a new style of seminars.

My yoga teacher, Shandor Remete (www.shadowyoga.com), said: "If you do your practice properly, no matter how much energy you expend, you should have more energy at the end than you did at the beginning." I thought, "That's great", so I experimented with that principle for ages. Eventually, I came up with the idea of doing everything creatively for 24 hours, regardless of how mundane the task. So that's what I did. I brushed my teeth differently, walked to my appointment differently, ate differently, came up with new ideas, spoke on the telephone in a new way. Everything. I worked for 23 hours solidly and had more energy at the end of the day than I did at the beginning. It works.

Experiments

How can I see the tasks I have to do as funny?

If this were in a sit-com with my favourite actors, how would this play out?

What if in ten years' time I was to tell the story of this moment now and it be one my funniest stories? What happened?

As vital as breathing

Recently I had an accident. I was riding my bike in London and the handlebars of my bike snapped in two. I took a big fall and broke my wrist in three places, cracked a rib and took a hit; 30 seconds earlier and it could have been a lot worse, but still the incident shook me.

I had been busy working on new projects. They were in development and needed maturing. Suddenly I couldn't write, dress myself, drive, cycle, carry anything... I had been riding high and this took the wind out of me. I lost my momentum and a few weeks later I found myself with a hole in my cash flow. For the first time in a long time I found myself with no work and absolutely nothing brewing and big bills coming in every day.

At first I was down about the whole thing. My confidence had taken a serious knock and I couldn't see any way out of my predicament. Every day things appeared worse and I could hear the wolves growling at the door. Not good. I knew something had to change, but what? I tried drumming up business, but with my energy low and feeling "disasterful", nothing was working out. This knocked my confidence even more. I couldn't sleep and that made things feel even worse. I had to do something and the only thing I could change was myself. However I felt, whatever nightmare scenarios my imagination played before me as fact, I had to change.

I started to work my imagination... to feel renewed success. I could feel the emergence of positive possibilities as sun on my face after a long winter. My bath at night became an immersive meditation into the warmth of potential. I would inevitably be awake at 3am so I spent hours visualizing and shifting the nightmares to positive films. I would start off remembering how it felt to play water polo, to be the strongest and fittest I could be, and to score the kinds of goals that no keeper could stop. Hard and uncompromising into the corner of the net. I felt the experience in my body, the elation of victory, the pleasure of success. I would then transfer that feeling to the events in my life... scanning the energetic horizon for clients and opportunities, walking through gardens plucking the low-hanging fruit pregnant with juice and knowing that each one was a project sweet-tasting and equally rich in nutrition and cash. At first my nightmare images would invade the sunshine films in my imaginings. I put at stop to it and forced myself to change my mind: "It's my mind. I know everything's going to be alright. Everything's going to be alright. It's my mind. I am the only one who can change it. I am the only one. I change." And so I would change the thoughts systematically. Every night the same thing would happen but over a week it became easier to shift the nightmare back to the sunshine. I would vary my water polo warm-up to other sports. Sometimes I would fire an arrow at a target a long way away and guide it with my consciousness until it hit the bullseye dead-centre. Sometimes

I would shoot basketball hoops. Sometimes I would make my seminars into delicious meals and serve them to new clients around a table, smelling the food and seeing them loving the taste and textures of my offerings, receiving back in abundance until all of us around the table were satisfied. Every day I would change the images subtly. I needed to keep them fresh. I needed to retain an interest and an enthusiasm for them and I needed to keep them free of my nightmares. I would bring those images and qualities into my day. I would experiment with walking invincibly, breathing invincibly, dressing successfully and scoring goals.

When you hold your breath underwater there is a moment when your body just has to breathe. It will do anything, break anything, push anything out of the way to break the surface of the water with your nose and mouth and breathe new life in. My need to turn my fortunes around was as vital to me as breathing.

There's an old expression I heard years ago – "don't feed the dragon". I stopped feeding my nightmares and they disintegrated. The world opened up and projects came to me almost immediately. I said "yes" to everything and the money rolled in. The world was sunny again. More than that, though, I realized that I made it shine, that I could make things happen whenever I wanted; I just had to focus in the right way... completely positively and absolutely... as absolutely as needing to breathe.

Surety brings results.

"Gently absolute"

My sister told me a story of when she was working as a teacher. She was in the staffroom one day incensed by something and talking to a couple of people: "This has to change... that has to change... students shouldn't have to put up with that", and so on. A wise teacher walked behind her and said, "Everything you say is true, Laura, but why do you need to shout?"

I was very touched by that story. I realized that I too was in the habit of needing a heightened moment or being on the brink to find this level of surety. It was a habit. I like rock climbing. Tying the cord around my waist to attach my chalk-bag when I climb always reminds me of tying my belt in karate. It is the same movement and my hands seem to find a pattern they have known for lifetimes. Once when I was climbing I began wondering if I could engage with it with the same absolute quality as I would were I fighting with sword and spear on the battlefield. Can we put the same absoluteness into peaceful activities as we would into war? What if we could? Where would that lead us?

If all experience translates, surely that means we only need to know the quality of engagement in one place to find it in another? Like the guy in my presentation skills course who could navigate his talk with the same quality as he attacked the racetrack on his motorbike. So I've started... and it's much nicer; definitely a higher "YES factor".

We can be "gently absolute".

Love trumps hate

A woman approached me after a seminar one day. She said: "I wonder if you can help. My son is doing really badly at French at school. He's doing well in everything else but he has exams coming up. I've tried getting him to work more but nothing's helping. Any ideas of what I could do?"

I asked: "What does he love?"

She said: "Rugby; he's mad about it. Watching, playing. The lot."

"Get him to do his French homework and decline his verbs while playing rugby... throwing a ball around."

"He can't do that – he's got to work!"

"How's that working out for you?"

"Erm... not very well."

"In that case try playing... get him to talk about his favourite team in French. Listen to French commentators talk through a game. Discuss tactics. Have him describe his most amazing match moments in French, while throwing a rugby ball around, and see how that works out."

She did so. He went from 17th out of 20 in the class to third out of 20 in one month. Why? Two reasons:

1. When we connect what we absolutely love with what we dislike, love always wins. It's so much brighter.
2. When we do this experientially it's like a quantum accelerator.

Love trumps hate.

Experiments

Where do you already know that quality of absolute commitment?

What are you absolutely sure about? That you breathe air? That you love football? That you have blonde hair?

Build a meditation for yourself where you experience places and qualities of surety.

Bring in the goals you wish to manifest.

Infuse them with this quality.

Draw in this possibility with the same lust as one who has been underwater and breaks the surface to engage with life-giving breath.

Do it non-stop for a minimum of eight days.

Report your findings on the Facebook page (Facebook: The 7 Questions to Find Your Purpose).

Principle Two: Be Persistent

"1 per cent inspiration, 99 per cent perspiration."

Pattabhi Jois

Choosing for something to happen in our lives is not a one-time thing. We have to repeat the same choice every day until it comes to fruition... a great wedding docs not mean a great marriage. Great relationships are made through showing up and giving the best of ourselves day in, day out. In the same way, to achieve our goals, further our Purpose and emerge into a lighter version of ourselves we have to stay with our choices longer... persistence.

A "critical mass" of actions

"Critical mass" is best known as the minimum amount of fissile material needed to maintain a nuclear chain reaction, but it is also a universal principle in nature. We are applying the term "critical mass" here to an area often neglected by people... their inner world of thoughts and beliefs. In the context of our process of development, it refers to "the amount of actions or input necessary to create lasting change".

There was a famous experiment where scientists observed the behaviour patterns of a particular species of monkey, simultaneously over a number of different islands. These monkeys were not in the habit of washing their food, so to test their ability to learn and adapt, scientists rolled potatoes in sand and left them on the beach. They then watched to see how long it would take before they worked out how to eat the food.

At first the monkeys ignored the food. It was not fit for consumption. After a while, however, the young, who habitually play and experiment with their world, discovered that they could wash and eat the potatoes. The mothers, who spend most of their time with the young, soon learned this behaviour and began to follow suit.

Before long, 60–70 monkeys had learned how to feed in this way, yet that knowledge had not spread through the tribe. The same was true when the figure crept up to 80 monkeys and even 90; each monkey had to make the discovery of washing their food individually. However, when the 100th monkey had learned that it could wash and eat the potatoes, monkeys from the same species on all the surrounding islands began spontaneously to clean their food and eat it. The distance between the islands was significant, ruling out the possibility of contact through sight and sound. For that species with that information, the critical mass necessary for knowledge to enter into their collective consciousness was 100 monkeys.

The principle of critical mass is as applicable to human beings as it is to nuclear reactions or monkeys. It may explain how and why the Berlin Wall came down peacefully overnight, and why political and social movements can take on a huge momentum with so few people visibly behind them.

I have witnessed the same phenomenon when delivering change programmes in organizations. Sometimes working with a department or team, I might see 20 people at a time for an hour and work through the whole department in a single day. There is little or no time for people to tell their colleagues about what happens in our session during that day and yet the questions which appear in the first few groups of the day have become a given to the groups at the end of the day. Critical mass has occurred.

In one project I was working with large numbers of people and high degrees of antagonism and negativity. They were angry at their organization – and since I was the only person in the room they could "blame" they did. Every day it was the same. The comments and behaviour seemed to grow in intensity, always revolving around the same themes. One day, while driving into work, I had what can only be called "an epiphany". I was listening to music and I began to hear the harmonic overtones in it. As I focused on the sound the world shifted colour. Everything became as silvered glass – the cars in front, the landscape, the cows in the field... after a few minutes the vision began to fade, but the feeling of ecstasy remained. I rounded the corner and the sky was perfectly blue with the exception of one deep-dark cloud covering one building in one area in a 180-degree vista – the building where I was headed. It was negativity, pure and simple. I knew beyond any doubt – and I knew the silvered state that was negative's negative.

I walked into the room in this state. There were over 100 people. Immediately some people started shouting: "I don't want to be here. What the hell am I doing here? This is a complete waste of money. There are services not being paid and you, some posh git from the South, are getting paid. It's a disgrace."

"Good morning," I said as I picked up the microphone. And we were off. I have never encountered negativity like it, a crowd so hostile and resistant. It made no difference. I was silver. It was my room. "They can be as negative as they want," I thought, but not in my room. "In here it's 'YES', it's positivity." Everything shifted that day. By lunchtime the vocal disrupters had become highly energized participants and by the end of the day there were cheers.

It was the straw that broke the camel's back... critical mass. There were over 100 training days still to be delivered on that project, yet those resistances never came up again.

Achieving change in an organizational context is about enough people focusing their intentions in a given direction in a short period of time – it takes 8–12 per cent of the population to do so. There also needs to be a momentum of activity so that the energy created by those people extends onto and ignites others around them. Like kick-starting a motorbike, it is important to push the pedal down fully – but equally important is the speed and power of the kick.

Internal critical mass also exists. If we generate a certain number and consistency of thoughts, sayings, feelings and actions we create a chain reaction that shifts our consciousness.

Achieving inner critical mass is about maintaining an absolute engagement with a given end (a goal or a new habit) for enough time with enough intensity. It's the basic principle of physical fitness... do enough exercise in a short enough time and things improve. Going to the gym once a month is not going to do it.

If we can sustain enough actions or focused intent on each of our goals we will achieve them. The more actions we take the more we learn about which actions to take. The more we think about achieving our goal the more those thoughts think... and send themselves back to us. It's a virtuous circle. We need to be persistent.

Experiments

There are hundreds of experiments in this book involving:

Visualization

Embodiment

Gaming

Absolute and positive intent.

Choose any of them... the ones that say "YES" to you eight, nine or ten out of ten and use them persistently for the amount of time we are told it takes to build new neural pathways – 33 days.

Share your learnings on Facebook (Facebook: The 7 Questions to Find Your Purpose).

Principle Three: Be Positive

Many years ago my wife and I attended a lecture by a man called Andrew Cohen. To paraphrase, he said that everything in life comes down to one question: Do we think life is fundamentally good, yes or no? If "yes", then whatever happens to us – we get hit by a bus and break both our legs – gives us the time to re-evaluate life, or read *War and Peace*, something good can come of it. Always. However, if we think "no", life is fundamentally not good, then however good life seems to be going, we always think the bubble is going to burst. The definition of optimism is believing that the future is going to be even better than the present. The definition of a pessimist is believing that it's going to be worse.

What if belief and choice are the same thing?

There's a true story about a man who had two sons. He spent spells in prison for theft and assault. He suffered from alcohol abuse and bouts of depression. One son grew up to be exactly the same as his father, spending time in detention centres, getting into fights and taking drugs. The other son took a different path and got a good job, raised a family and so on.

Both sons were asked the same question: "How do you account for the way you turned out?" They both gave exactly the same answer: "What do you expect with a father like mine?"

One son saw his father as an example, while the other saw him as a warning. The difference between the two sons was a fundamental choice: do I choose to make the best out of life regardless of what it throws at me, yes or no? One chose "yes" the other "no".

What if we decide that today's a "bad" day? When we walk across town in the mood our decision causes, what do we notice? Do we look at the headline of a newspaper advertising famine and crisis? A broken shop window? Graffiti? The dark rainclouds? The person who walks directly in front of us, nearly tripping us up? We may be convinced that it's a bad day, but are we right?

Do you believe that the world is "bad" today, or do you choose it?

What if we chose today to be a "good" day, what would we notice? The mother playing with her child? The couple gently holding hands at the bus stop? That top you like in the window at half-price? The driver waving another car through? We might be convinced that it really is a good day. Are we right? Again, do you believe that the world is "good" today, or do you choose?

There's an exercise I do with groups where I ask them to look around the room and notice everything red or red-ish. I then ask them to shut their eyes and tell me what they saw that was green. People call out one or two things. When they open their eyes again they see that there are a whole host of green things that they simply had not noticed before. They were always there, but while they were looking for red they do not see green. Proust said that "we do not see the world as it is, we see the world as we are". Belief and choice are the same thing. When we choose to see red, we believe that is the predominant colour.

Choice and focus

When you take anything – a rock, a tree or a human being – and look at it on a sub-atomic level, we are all made up of light – of particles of energy. There was an experiment conducted in the United States to find out if there is any pattern to the movement of electrons. The reasoning behind the experiment was: if we can discover the nature of the building blocks for matter, we can discover a pattern to everything solid. That is, if I understand how a brick responds to the world then

I will know how a building is likely to respond and then a town and ultimately a planet, and so on.

The movements of a single electron were mapped on a screen. To find a place to start, the scientists decided they would see how many times the electron moved to the top of the screen during its seemingly random movements. Immediately, the electron began moving upwards. They marked down the results. Next they wanted to know how many times it moved to the left. The electron started moving to the left. Next to the right – it moved to the right, and so on. The scientists soon started to realize that wherever they chose to look affected the electron's flow. It follows then that if the little pieces of matter respond to our choices, when those little pieces make big pieces, they too will respond to our focused will.

Your focus steers the flow of matter. Your choices affect your world and the world.

Imagine then, if you could choose to consistently say "YES" at an eight, nine or ten out of ten to life through your actions, in your relationships and through your work. What if there were a critical mass of people making positive choices everyday... All electrons flowing in positive directions... How would that affect your world and that of others?

You can't action a "not". Complete every "no" with a "yes".

If you were a tightrope-walker on a wire, halfway between the platforms, and started telling yourself "don't fall, don't fall", what are you focusing on? Falling, right? If we focus on "balance" or "serenity" or "equilibrium" we achieve more of that. You can't action a "not".

When has saying "don't panic" ever stopped someone panicking?

Whenever we give ourselves a negative instruction our minds simply focus on what it can picture or create. When we picture being afraid more than being confident we send our electrons in that direction and end up encouraging the outcome we would most like to avoid. We are the imaginations of ourselves in action, or "imagin-actions". You, me and everyone else are just big walking plasma screens playing out whatever our imagin-actions direct, so it's important to find ways of directing it well.

I once had a coaching client who wanted to lose weight. She was unhappy with her shape and had been dieting for months to little effect. I asked her some questions to find out about her relationship to food and meals. She told me, "I eat a lot of salad and vegetables, but what I really want is chocolate cake and biscuits."

"So, in fact, every time you sit down to eat, you are in denial and sacrifice?"

"Well, yes, I suppose so."

"The trouble is," I replied, "you can't action a 'not', and your whole dietary system is based on 'not eating', rather than any positive intention of becoming slim."

What she really wanted was to look good for her cousin's wedding in six months' time. So we created a positive cycle for her – rather than saying "no" to the chocolate cake, she changed this to say "yes" to her positive image of herself at her cousin's wedding."

She looked great and happy on the big day.

Action a "yes" over a "not" simply by reformulating it in your mind. For example, "not fearful" = "being confident". A simple way of looking at this idea is to take the metaphor of a battery. Electricity naturally flows from negative to positive; "no" is negative, "yes" is positive. To keep us in a flow of progress and to move forward with our Purpose, we must constantly move toward the positive. The moment we stay in the negative zone the current stops and our energy stagnates and dies. Completing every "no" with a "yes" simply moves the energy forward and we progress positively.

Is this a process of denial? No, it's a process of completion. Positive living accounts for the negative. It is a part of life. Identify and see it, yes, then move on. Notice that the minus or negative sign "-" is half the positive sign "+"... it's only halfway there. This notion is just another way of looking at the "YES factor". Imagine that all your "not" thoughts are in the two, three or four zone and all your most positive ones are in the eight, nine or ten zone. Only action eights and above. As we do this we become naturally more effective. After a while these thoughts become second nature and we start to train ourselves to cultivate a "YES" outlook.

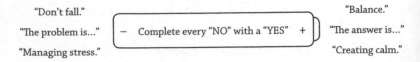

"Don't fall."

"The problem is..."

"Managing stress."

− Complete every "NO" with a "YES" +

"Balance."

"The answer is..."

"Creating calm."

Memory and foresight are equally powerful

Often when people meditate and visualize the realization of their goals they focus entirely on the future: "This will happen", "It will feel like this", "I'm going to have such and such". That's great but we have to connect it to what we already know. We have to find the pieces of Velcro in our past which connect to the ones in our future. We have to find where we already know the experience of what we are creating.

It's also useful to remind ourselves regularly of why we want the things that we have chosen in our goals. What is it we love about them? Why? What's the experience we think we will have, having it? Where do I know that already? I've had the experience before and... like when a sniffer dog is given something to smell and searches until it finds the same again, we can sense that experience in its new wrapping.

Experiments

- Look at one of the goals you wrote down earlier. Name the experience.

- Where have you felt that before? What does it remind you of? Remember. Feel the experience. Feed off it.

- Now, start your visualization of that same experience in the new context and shape of your goals. Circulate your breathing... the memory into the new, the new into the memory... like a person playing the didgeridoo. Breathe one in and one out until the two are one.

- Repeat often.

- Use the "YES factor" religiously. That's what it's for.

- Make an eight, nine or ten music or YouTube playlist.

- If, when you think about your goals you predominantly visualize them, try using your other senses... What would it taste like? What will I hear and feel? What would it feel like in my body? How does it feel to touch?

Touch those things, feel those things, taste those things,
hear those things...
...and then you'll see them.

Principle Four: Be in Action

"He who deliberates fully before taking a step will spend the rest of
his life on one leg."

Chinese proverb

There's an exercise I run with groups to develop spontaneity, creativity
and elasticity of thinking. I call it the Object Game. We stand in a circle
and place an object in the centre. This could be anything... a bottle, a
rolled-up pad of paper, a watering can, anything. One by one someone
comes into the centre of the circle and, without speaking, picks up the
object and starts to use it as something different. The rest of the group has
to guess what the object has become. Groups often start with uses similar
to the original shape – for example, a bottle being used as a telescope or
a vase. It then grows and develops. The bottle might become a gear lever
for a car or a lightbulb. I then encourage the group to use the object in
ways which have no relationship to its shape, material or function. The
bottle could become the handle for a door to a castle, a pet dog or a tree.
Over the years I have noticed that there are three types of people:

1. People who jump in and have a go. These people have the "that-
   reminds-me-of" button firing in their heads. When another person
   is using the object they let it remind them of something else and
   have a never-ending stream of ideas to try out.
2. People who have an idea and want to work out exactly what they're
   going to do before taking part. They watch other people, study the
   reactions of the group, occasionally take part and often have their
   idea actioned by someone else before jumping into the ring.
3. People who don't have ideas and don't know how to get any going.

Before I carry on let me just say that these tend to be people's default positions. Far be it for me to say that people are not capable or willing to change their approach, everything in life is flexible and up for grabs. A default position means that this is the approach they have fallen into the habit of adopting and without-considering-another-option has become their usual way of being. They then tend to say "I'm a [this] kind of a person" or "I'm a [that] kind of a person". They have made up their minds about who they are – and that is a dangerous place to be. When we fix an idea about ourselves we tend not to deviate much from that. Whether that choice is conscious or unconscious is irrelevant. The effect is the same.

I like to encourage people to step into the circle and grab the object before they have an idea. Inevitably, the moment they approach it or pick it up something comes to them. It is often unexpected and makes them and others smile. It is their action, their intention, their engagement which kick-starts their mind. They are literally saying to themselves "I'm going to have an idea in a moment", and of course they do. In our careful pre-planned world where making a mistake is seen as worse than having a go, we need to adopt this mindset more overtly.

There is a Zen saying that "the mind is a wonderful servant and a terrible master". When we engage fully the mind becomes the servant of intent and it furnishes us with what we need. The mind is an amazing suggestion box and the subconscious is like a cinema, it can show horror films or inspirational life-changing tales and it can do this non-stop. If we go to the mind before engaging with intent it will come up with one possibility after another ad infinitum. We never really know which course of action is the best for us and the more choice we have the more debilitating it can feel. We have to jump into the circle, pick up the object and have a go. Our mind will fall into line and a string of possibilities will ensue.

- Perfection is a trap. It's the opposite of spontaneity, which means we sacrifice presence and therefore life.
- Underpreparing is often a defence – "the only reason I failed was because..."
- An eight is good enough.
- When we're in, we are alive in it. We work it out.
- We have to act. We have to engage. We have to try things before we know what to do completely.
- The way we play the game is the way we are in life.
- Which one of the three types of player (of the Object Game) is closest to you?

Nothing happens without action. Tepid action breeds inconclusive results, which lead to doubt. This is where most people who want to live their Purpose get stuck. They do the seven questions, feel a sense of liberation and possibility, engage with the exercises for focusing their goals and then... let the entropy of past habits leach their newfound sense of empowerment away until it disappears like wine in the sand, saying things like:

"Life just got in the way."

"My Purpose isn't practical."

"If only I had more money, more time, more... more."

"I can't just quit my job."

Blah, blah, blah. As Richard Bach said, "Argue for your limitations and sure enough they're yours." Muhammad Ali wasn't the greatest when he started saying "I am the greatest", but then he was. If he had started saying "I'm pretty good and I hope to get there one day, with a following wind, if all goes well", would he have become an icon for a generation?

My daughter has a beautiful singing voice. When she was a baby she could cry with a force Aretha Franklin would be proud of. Now she sings like an angel. We were in the car going somewhere and she started singing a solo she had performed at school. When she hit a sustained high note, she sounded somewhere between a classical soprano and a blues singer on a great day. It was arresting. One of the passengers, an elderly lady, laughed. Immediately my daughter stopped singing and wouldn't start again despite repeatedly being asked. I had a conversation with her about it:

"No, I don't want to sing, it's stupid."

"Why? "

"Because she laughed."

"Do you know why she laughed?"

"No."

"Because in the family she came from, if she did anything that stood out, if she excelled in any way that was different to the 'family norm', people teased her... and she just took the habit. She doesn't even know why she's doing it. It just seems normal to her. It's her background but it doesn't have to be yours. Don't let anybody rule when you sing and when you don't. You rule you. You sing because you sing."

Sometimes we make it a cultural necessity to argue for our limitations. We even ensure this continuance by supporting a media which plays a game of attacking people who excel publicly, as if somehow it's wrong to stand out. In other words, projecting onto others our fear of being seen, either privately in our relationships or publicly by being complicitous with the belief system. It's the same in our organizations. In what we wear. In so many of our behaviours.

A study was done to see which organizational cultures were the most conservative. In other words, which organizations had a culture where people did not deviate from the established norms? They studied businesses, public services, fan groups and supporters, hobbyists and so on. The most conservative of all those studied was the Hell's

Angels. Big, biker dudes with bushy beards, tattoos, leather jackets and Harley Davidsons. I was amazed. When I found out why it made me laugh... you couldn't turn up to a Hell's Angels gathering wearing a suit, driving a Ford and sipping a latte. There were cultural norms that were so entrenched that people retained them rigidly... even in groups established to live outside cultural norms. Collusion is collusion wherever it's found.

Of course, there is nothing wrong with sitting firmly in the middle of our cultural establishment, but that has nothing to do with either our actions or our choices. Our Purposeful goals may seem radical, which means "at the root of". In other words, being "radical" really means going back to the root or heart of what we want. In this sense our Purposeful goals are always radical. They are coming home and your home is yours. You sing because you sing. Are we here to perpetuate the status quo or to enrich it with the possibilities born of our uniqueness?

What makes it harder sometimes is that we are empathically connected. We literally feel the prevailing winds of opinion from those around us. A baby doesn't realize that it is distinct from the beings around it. It has no idea if what it feels is from itself or from the people around. It picks up everything. That's us. We're babies. We never lose this sensitivity, we just learn different ways of processing it. And because we "hear" those around us so compellingly we don't know if the choices we make are as a result of us or the prevailing winds. The beauty of a choir is not that everybody sings the same note, it is the harmony that is struck when everyone sings their part, together. When we live our Purpose we call on our truest, purest voice. It can be gravelly and bluesy or a choirboy's. What matters is that it is our voice. Harmonies enhance the music. Being the same adds no value.

When we sing a harmony we have to hear both the sound of our own voice and the music as it plays inside our minds. When we can add "listening to everyone else" at the same time, we enjoy singing harmonies. I use harmonization as a way of learning how to listen to oneself and enjoy others at the same time. To be centred and together.

Experiments

- How do you stay in touch with yourself and also listen to others? How often do you remember/forget? How can you up your average?

- Watch "how to harmonize" videos on YouTube.

- Experiment with random harmonization when listening to music on the radio.

- All experience translates so... how could you harmonize your movements with those around? Your speech patterns?

Look at your goals:

- How much good can come from you realizing this goal? Who will benefit? In how many different ways? What might be the long-term impact?

- Are your goals very different to what you thought you wanted or are they radically different?

Time limits

Whereas 25 years ago I used to give people two hours to complete an exercise, now I give them 15 minutes and they get better results.

Time limits are fantastic. They focus the mind. They create a "must" – "this must get done". And they give us an end point. If when we are skiing or riding a bike we look at the ground directly in front of us when we're turning, we'll crash. Instead, we look ahead at the place we want to reach. Our feet, our bodies, our weight all collaborate to reach this point. A time limit has the same effect. Set a time and date for when you will have achieved your goal, or a time for when you will have agreed the actions you are going to take. What's the amount of time that feels doable? Short enough that it galvanizes, long enough that it does not stress you out?

Yes, you read correctly – a time and a date. Even if it's several months or years into the future. Something happens when we set a time. It feels more real. Saying to ourselves "I'll have this done by 8pm on the 17th" galvanizes us into self-edit mode so we focus on the essential. We become specific, like following a ski instructor and turning when he or she turns instead of doing so at any time we like. It focuses intent... all our horses pulling in the same direction, as we shout "yah!" (or something equally cowboy-like).

Life is time limited.
Every goal is a life.

Experiments

Choose an area of life:

- By when will you have decided your goal?

- By when will you have achieved this goal?

- By when will you have worked out your action plan?

- By when will you have started?

- And so on...

"I know what my goals are but I don't know how
to go about achieving them."

What if you did? What if somewhere you knew exactly what to do?
There's a great game you can play where one person asks another how
to do something they don't know how to do and they have to give an
answer that makes some kind of sense.

Q: What don't you know how to do?

A: Change the carburettor on a car.

Q: How do you change the carburettor on a car?

A: I'd unscrew the screws and pipes into the carburettor, buy another
one and then put the pipes and screws back in.

Gradually, the tasks become more and more complex or far out... "How would you create free abundant energy for the planet?" or "How would you achieve faster-than-light travel?" Yet, once people are in their flow they come out with answers which can be remarkably astute. By answering a question even when you don't know what the answer is, you actually find out that you know enough to find out the answer.

I was climbing an overhanging rock-face and trying to get to the top and failing miserably. I tried everything I knew in as many ways as I could muster, to no avail. Knowing that I only had one or two attempts left before my arms gave way completely, I decided to "google myself" on the assumption that I knew somewhere subconsciously how to get to the top. I asked myself: "If you were an amazing climber, you might do something like..." A shape and an energy formed in my mind and before I knew it I was over the crux of the route and at the top. It happened faster than my consciousness could collect. I didn't know exactly how I had made it but... I was at the top. It was categorical. I knew but I didn't know I knew. Do I really need to know how the Google algorithm works to trust in the results of my Internet search or do I simply type a word in the box and press "return"?

If belief and choice really are the same thing then building belief is an important part of action:

Who else has done something similar to anything you have identified in your goals?

How did they go about doing it?

What would be your way of doing the same thing?

What feels achievable, fun and exciting? How could it become more fun, achievable or exciting?

Experiments

- What if you knew exactly how to achieve your goals? If you did, you might do something like... you'd contact.... you'd chat with.... you'd have a go at...

- Write down your answers.

- Place at one end of the room a picture or object that symbolizes one of your goals. Now write the numbers 1–10 on separate pieces of paper and lay them out on the floor like stepping stones leading to your goal. Keep a pencil in your hand.

- Which number on the scale is closest to where you currently feel you are in relation to that goal?

- Stand on that number.

- Look one step ahead. It's so easy to take a step, to move up a point.

- Take a step. How does that feel? What's going on here? Look back at your previous number. What got you here? Make a note of any answer that comes to you on the number at your feet.

- When you feel like it, look at the next number in the chain and repeat the process.

- When you have finished you should have the beginnings of a list of actions, which your unconscious is telling you takes you from where you are now to where you choose to be.

- Repeat the same process, replacing your goal with your personal hero. As you approach him or her, what are the actions you feel you need to take? The changes you might need to make? The beliefs and ideas you might need to drop? What's going to make you make that journey complete?

Most people know what to do but don't do it.

Principle Five: Be Game

Viola Spolin, the godmother of improvisational theatre, used gaming principles to help people move beyond their fears and accept a new reality for themselves. Essentially, she says that when we find ourselves in any "performance" dynamic most people enter the "approval/disapproval paradigm". It could be a presentation, being with our spouses, our kids or around the dinner table. This essentially means that people are asking themselves "what do I need to do to win approval and avoid disapproval?". They then amend their behaviour accordingly. To put it another way, we have a whole keyboard of possibilities available to us, yet we only play the six notes in the middle. There are some great tunes there and lots of variations but it's not Tchaikovsky – and, more to the point, it does not even begin to touch our potential.

She said that we could work away at the paradigm, trying to eek out an extra note here and there, or, alternatively, we could do it through games. When we play we invent a whole new set of rules for ourselves. "Usual behaviour" goes out of the window and we open to all our senses and all our perceptions. A much greater part of the keyboard becomes available to us and we happily explore it.

Happily explore it.

In the process we "discover" more of who we are and what we can be, do and have. Those discoveries, if made conscious, can enter into our way of being and bring new insight and habits.

The power of embodiment

As an actor I love embodiment... to explore an idea through trying it on and being it. There can be surprising and very interesting results. I was in a meeting one day with a large organization; I was playing with being fabulously wealthy. I put shoes on that made me feel crisper and sharper. I rode my bike to the meeting "wealthily". I wrote my name as I checked into their building imagining I was a nobleman signing with a feather quill. The lift was a "carriage". Then I was in the meeting. I was fabulously wealthy and "knew" that I didn't need to work but I was happy to help these people, and so on.

At one point in the meeting, when some work had been established, I normally would have gone into a stage in the conversation where we organize the scale of the courses to be run, some next-step stages and then end the meeting. For some reason, though, I didn't fill this gap in the conversation; I didn't get out at that stop. I felt like waiting and the conversation started to move in another unexpected direction. I was still being fabulously wealthy when the lead guy in the room said: "I hope you don't mind, but we have a chunk of money we have to spend before we go into next year's budget. Would you mind if we paid you this and you work out how much time you can give us?"

"Er... yes that sounds fine."

"Oh and would it be OK if we paid you this immediately?"

"Hmm, let me think about this... big budget, paid up front and I design whatever I like. Er, yes that's perfect, thank you."

Playing fabulously wealthy had led to feeling fabulously wealthy, which led to a lot of money coming in very quickly.

I coached a woman before giving a talk once. She was extremely bright, had a brilliant mind and there was no question that she could deliver as well as anybody in the business; however, she had had a traumatic experience in the past and was terrified of standing in front of a group of her peers. Necessity had overtaken her and the talk was in an hour's time. As we were walking to an empty meeting room to start her coaching session I found out that she loved to ride horses. I decided that we didn't have enough time to create a fresh mindset about her up-and-coming challenge; instead, it was much easier to play horsie. I got her to pretend to be sitting in the saddle as she rehearsed her talk. Every time she made her point I snorted, giving my best horse impersonation. I do a mean horse. When she made her conclusion, she pulled back on the reins as if to make the horse back up, and so on.

I saw her talk. She shone. She has given countless presentations since then without a moment's hesitation. Through "playing horsie" we made more progress in an hour that we would have in a month in a normal training context.

Visualization

The subconscious mind does not distinguish between qualities of experience. We can taste success, smell resolution, hear achievement. We can take an experience in one circumstance and apply it to another, giving us endless manifestation games.

When I was last moving house there was a delay in receiving some official planning paperwork. This went on for months, despite my chasing. When things started to get to a stage where there would be serious financial penalties if we could not complete on time, I made up a very specific visualization: In my mind I took the energy of my old house and saw it as a bowl of Greek yoghurt. The energy of the new house became raspberry coulis. I then took the official body, which had spent so long not signing and sending my form, in hand as a huge wooden spoon and leaned over the imaginary bowl to mix them all together. Focused intent. I mixed them until they were blended and I could feel a shift. We received our documentation a few days later. There are people who will say that is ridiculous. There are people who will prove its veracity with quantum physics. If we listen to others we "think" something is true or not. If we experiment and experience for ourselves, we "know". Make up your own mind.

We can visualize with our eyes closed in meditation or we can do it in movement, cooking, driving or any other activity.

Be game and visualize:
- It's the fastest form of learning.
- It accelerates critical mass.
- It is a self-sustaining energy source.
- It releases unbounded creativity.
- It is a perfect route of exploration.

Experiments

We could talk about playing games or we could play them. Here are some suggestions to get you going:

- How will you feel when you are living your Purpose nine or ten out of ten? Spend a whole day being that. Brushing your teeth on a nine, drinking tea on a nine, walking to work on a nine, having phone calls on a nine, listening on a nine, cooking dinner on a nine, making love on a nine.

- When you embody your goal or your Purpose, how do you stand or move differently? If you find that you are no longer holding certain "fixed positions" or expressions, try experimenting with holding those fixed positions on purpose. Activating them and releasing them. What do they remind you of? What gift can you give to that memory to forgive it?

- Take each one of your goals. Make them balloons in your mind. Fill them up with fun one day, light the next, ease the next.

- Experiment with other qualities, fill them up with sexual ecstasy, mountain air, the laugh of a child.

- Watch a video of your favourite sports person winning a medal or a trophy. Exchange places with them in your mind.

Imagine having realized one of your goals while receiving the gold medal or raising the cup above your head.

- Take the next six months in your mind, pave each week with gold, sprinkle laughter liberally over the days, watch plants, trees and rivers spring up around the path, breathing life into everything you do. See yourself putting golden energy into the earth as you walk the path and then receiving it back again with interest every other step.

- Write a newspaper review of having achieved your goal. Write one, two or three paragraphs and make sure that it makes you laugh. Read it every couple of weeks.

Next time you cook a meal, imagine you are making one of your goals. Make it taste and feel perfect, be aware of any pull or intuition to do things differently from how you might immediately expect. Does it need to be sweeter or more savoury? Are there extra ingredients to add? Do you need to change the proportions or consistency? When you eventually eat the food, how does it make you feel? If you had to translate anything about the experience of cooking it to your plans for achieving your goal, what would you say?

- Make up five new visualizations and share them on Facebook (Facebook: The 7 Questions to Find Your Purpose).

Principle Six: Clear the Past

When we are not reaching or progressing to our goals it's often because of a story we perpetually tell ourselves based on our past and one that is restricting our future.

It's a bit like we're looking down a long, sweeping road, which stretches from where we are now to where our goals lie – our pot of gold. We can walk that path, listening to some great tunes, hand in hand with the people we love, munching our favourite food and skipping every step of the way. Instead, some people look behind them at the road along which they have come and see all the potholes, difficult weather and places where they broke down. When they look again at the road ahead they cut and paste these images along the path, obscuring their goal and making the road ahead arduous and difficult. Why does the past have to be the future? We are the only thing the past, present and future have in common. And we can change.

Letting go and learning the lessons of the past is how we equalize it. We have to forgive ourselves, others and the world in order to move on. We truly forgive when we are able to give to that person, or event, openheartedly. Forgiveness is a gift.

The gift

Many years ago I worked with the Original Shakespeare Company – a wonderful and extraordinary experience. What a gift. The company specialized in performing "his majesty's" plays in, you guessed it, the original way. In Shakespeare's day there were no printing presses. Scripts had to be written by hand. It was too time-consuming to write the whole play out for every member of the cast, so instead the actors were only given their lines. There was a three-word cue before they needed to speak. They had three words to come on stage and three words to go off. They did not know who said these words or when, just that these were your cue. They performed a different play every night and so there were no rehearsals. Instead, the "stage directions" were written into the script. For example, when the word "you" was in your lines it meant that your character would be in a formal setting, addressing somebody of higher status or a distance from another person on stage; where you were to say "thou", you were physically closer or more intimate with another. The only rehearsals were for fights or dances, and the first time one worked with the other actors was at the performance when we were told, this is your mother, this is your lover, this guy is your best friend and so on.

I had never worked in this way before and I wanted to experience it fully. I was playing Valentine in *The Two Gentlemen of Verona*. I did not know the play and decided not to cheat by reading the full version. While learning my lines in the garden I discovered that Valentine has to flee Verona to protect the love of his life, Sylvia. His best friend Proteus swears an oath to protect her in his absence. While hiding in the forest Valentine witnesses his friend trying to force Sylvia to make love to him. Valentine is incensed as he pulls his friend away. Furious, he gives a speech full of anger and outrage. The next cue, however, are the words "...forgive me Valentine", and he does completely.

I thought to myself: "He must have an amazing speech here for Valentine to forgive him so readily. He must have really pulled it out of the bag." The problem was that, as a modern actor, I am familiar with many of Shakespeare's great speeches. If there was a speech like "the quality of mercy is not strained" I would probably know it but I didn't know any speeches from *The Two Gentlemen of Verona*. What was I to do? I decided that the only way of tackling the problem was to create a moment of unconditional forgiveness at that point. Having no idea of what was said before, what other choice did I have? I played Valentine with a beautiful crucifix around his neck and planned to give it to Proteus as a symbol of my faith. It also meant that I had to be able to enter into a state of unconditional forgiveness at will, whenever I wanted and whatever the circumstances.

For two weeks I paced up and down my garden diving deeply into forgiveness purely and completely, with no warm-up. I did it until I could do it on cue.

A few weeks later, I was on stage at the Temple of Diana in the ancient Roman city of Jerash in Jordan. The evening sky was red. Two minutes before the performance a thin film of desert sand rained down onto the stage. The music sounded and the play began. It was a whirlwind... electric. Not knowing was intoxicating. Knowing one's bit and seeing how it fitted into the whole was like an epiphany. As the sky darkened and the play wore on, the moment came when I had to tear Proteus from the protesting form of my Sylvia. As I finished my eruption of outrage, Proteus simply said "forgive me Valentine". I was stunned and in the waiting silence I entered the state of unconditional forgiveness grown in my garden, removed my crucifix, placed it around his neck and forgave him.

I then "discovered" the rest of the play. In the remaining ten minutes Valentine manages to get every character in the play forgiven. I had not realized, studying the script, that this was what was happening. I had assumed the final few pages were simply a convenient way of wrapping up the story neatly. However, having performed the unconditional act of forgiveness it seemed to me that Valentine then carried that energy, spreading it liberally and bringing harmony back to the world of the play. Valentine... lover.

My yoga teacher Shandor Remete says: "You do your yoga so that you can find your inner strength in the moments when you need it such as the loss of a parent. If you cannot find your strength then, all your practice has been a complete waste of time." For me, experience is yoga. Whether through being on stage, writing, playing sport, being a parent, a husband, cooking, dancing. It's all experience and all experience translates.

I have an amazing friend called Michael Reece. He talks about acceptance and forgiveness in a beautiful way. He says that he sees life as if he is sitting on a tube train. All the moments are like stops on the train. They could be unpleasant, such as arguments with loved ones, or they could be wonderful; they are all stops where you have a choice to get out or not. "When we feel upset by someone, whether we say anything or not," he says, "we walk around having that argument in our head over and over again." We stew on it and think about all the things we could have, should have said. "That", Michael says, "is getting out at that stop." It's a "stop" we can choose to get out at or stay in. He says that when he has an argument with his partner he often says to himself: "I could get out here and stay with this argument but... I think I'll stay in and pass it by." It's a wonderful technique and way of looking at things. I thoroughly recommend it.

We can look at the road we have travelled in this way, seeing the points of difficulty we may have experienced and realizing that we didn't need to get out at that stop any more than a baby needed to give up trying to walk when it fell down time after time. We can realize that we are still here but that with every stop where we decided to get out, we left a part of ourselves. Getting out at a stop means we have stopped allowing that part to grow. We must bring it up to date, to reassemble ourselves so that we can move on.

Give is the heart of for-give-ness. Recognizing that each of these stops holds a gift of learning for us brings allowance... releasing the handbrake. Truly acknowledging the lesson is like letting manure permeate the soil – it can smell bad at first but it gives nutrients back and helps new life to form. It's good. However, just receiving the gift of the moment is not enough, we release ourselves to move on by *giving a gift* to the people, circumstances and events of that moment. The nature of the gift is not as important as the act of openhearted giving, but it may hold insight.

For example, in my 20s my girlfriend, now my wife, left her native France to live with me in London. It was a wrench for her. A few months after she arrived I was playing Shylock in *The Merchant of Venice* touring around the UK, which meant that I was away from home for long stretches. Not knowing anyone in London or having a job, this was understandably hard for her. Coupled with that I was asked to hold dates for significant roles in films for long periods of time and couldn't make plans, which was frustrating and destabilizing for us both. Eventually, she said that my life as an actor was not conducive to the way she wanted to live and that if I wanted to continue she would return to France. Give it up or give me up. I stopped focusing on my acting and together we developed our company YES.

I love my wife, YES has been an extraordinary adventure and we have two wonderful children. Staying together was the right choice for me. However, giving up something I love wasn't. A part of me "got out" at that station. This was a significant junction and a decision that has affected a myriad of choices both personal and professional since then. So, using my own approach... what has that moment taught me? That I am more than my job. That one's abilities and loves can have many forms and satisfactions. I have learned volumes about the human experience, about learning itself, personal development, teaching, speaking, writing stories that drive change, of holding hands with another, not knowing what is best but forging a path together nonetheless. I have learned about commitment, professionalism, connection, geopolitics and corporate entities, the world's new nation states and, of course, about relationship. The lessons are multitudinous and I am grateful for every one... there is also one other – that no choice involving sacrifice is ever completely fulfilling or nourishing for the soul. It is incomplete. For 25 years a part of me stayed in that station and no amount of learning could move it on.

Forgiveness is beyond learning and in many ways beyond the reasoning of the conscious mind.

I decided to look back on that time and give her, and it, a gift. I did not know what gift was appropriate so I sought around in my imagination to find a quality that fitted; that felt complete. I had no attachments to what the gift might be, whether I could create it or of its scale. It could have been a book, a dog or breakfast in bed. The unconscious mind speaks in metaphors and symbols, many of which are multi-layered. When I felt into it the gift that came to me was a chalet in the mountains financed by my acting. I made the resolution to make the gift. I felt it become complete and then let it be. Something shifted inside and I knew something new had begun. A part of me got on the train and left the station.

We are currently looking to move house and country.

Sometimes, the places where we get off the train are not just the difficult ones. When I was a child my hero was Tarzan. For me he epitomized the best in people and the best in nature. I gained so much from having this icon as a role model for me... the love of nature, fitness, a comfort with operating by a different set of principles to many of the people one meets, acting, climbing, an appreciation for innate nobility and much more besides. What could be wrong with that? Nothing, right?

As an experiment I decided to do the same ritual with Tarzan as I had with my choice as an actor and facilitator. I started by looking at the lessons I have learned from him... as mentioned. Then I decided to offer a gift to him... or rather to offer a gift to what he symbolized for me.

My image of him changed. His knife – a plastic version of which I used to put between my teeth and fight an imaginary crocodile with – dissolved and was replaced by a pen... and he was smiling. I chose to give through my experiment with this life. To create books, films and so on – pass it all on. This made a lot of sense to me. It represented a growing up of sorts; a connection between my present and my past, which holds no baggage or weight. It had been equalized and I felt better and stronger because of it. I call this process – The Gift.

As an actor I entered the corporate world. I carried no preconceptions, no ambition or wish to control into that environment. I was a man born into one environment and placed in the jungle of another with only his training from his home to call upon. It's been great fun. It's meant I've done things differently by choice and by accident. I love that. I wouldn't give back those years for anything. Now I do it to create not to survive, hence the knife changing to the pen. It's a wonderful completion for me. Very quiet.

Playing with the subconscious is extremely freeing and ultimately intimate. The symbols and compositions are subtle and rich. They merit close digestion. I share mine here in the hope that you realize the intimate pleasure of your own encounters with the part of you that knows more than you know.

Experiments

This is a build on the earlier exercise

Future:

- Place at one end of a room something – a picture or an object – that iconizes one of your Purposeful goals.

- Place the numbers 1–10 on the floor leading up to your icon.

- Stand where you think you are currently in relation to that.

- Move one step up. What did that feel like? Look back to where you came from. How did you get there? What steps did you take? Write down your answers.

- Repeat until you are as high as you can go.

Past:

- Stand where you think you are on your journey in relation to your goal, as in the previous experiment.

- Now look at the journey of your past, the path you have taken to get to where you are. Walk it through, making a note of the places you "got out" of the train. What were the testing moments? What were the decisions you took because of them?

- Write those down on a card and place them on your path.

- Now walk the floor again. Stop at those moments. What lessons did they teach? What happened as a result? Knowing what you now know, what advice would you give to the person you were back then? Write down what you find.

- Gift this person, event or circumstances. If you were to give wholeheartedly to this person, event or circumstances, what would you give?

- Give it. In your mind and in an action if you feel like it.

- When it's given, pick up that card and get back on the train.

- Move to the next stop and repeat.

Conclusion

"Opussing"

"Opussing" is the word I use to describe the conscious creation of one's life as an evolving work – where art and science meet. It means your life is important, not just for you but for the whole and for all time... opussing.

Stage 1: You have done the seven questions. You know the Purpose you serve. You can turn your intentions into actions and your actions into habits. You can become the finer version of yourself.

What next?

Stage 2: You can create your life as an opus... a work of art, a collected works of Purposeful offerings. There may only be space for three sentences in the *Book of Life* but you have all the time and space you need. You can make it all. I believe that all great artists and scientists live on the edge of conscious creation and discovery... always becoming the next stage of expansion.

Stage 3: Is when a critical mass of people on the planet live their Purpose and consciously create their opus. What happens then? What is a world like when there are hundreds of thousands, even millions, of people living their highest choices as opposed to colluding with the hand they feel society has dealt them – a free, empowered choice as opposed to an unconscious, compromised one?

Purposeful people have always changed the world and they always will. In every generation the expression of their Purpose changes but the quality remains the same. A small number of highly motivated, well-meaning, visionary people defy all obstacles inherent in the status quo to make the reality of their higher mind's eye a reality in the world. Gandhi is my personal favourite. You can see his influence echoed out in the world in a myriad of different ways... with Martin Luther King, Jr, Muhammad Ali, the Dakota Pipeline protests, Jeremy Gilley's Peace One Day, Bob Marley, Mother Theresa, Nelson Mandela and John Lennon, to name but a few. The influence goes way beyond anything we can even map. These figures are well known and there are thousands who change the world in less public but equally profound ways everyday. It is easier to identify it with doctors, nurses and care workers, but I have seen the same quality in people working in the world's major institutions (the United Nations, NATO, the EU, and so on), in business (Coca-Cola, Unilever, Procter & Gamble, Google), with teachers, rubbish collectors, chefs, actors, dancers and even occasionally in politicians. Purposeful people are everywhere. They are people who care, who give themselves, who are ignited by contribution and who go beyond their perceptions of themselves to give more and live more.

There are, of course, a lot of people who are not at all Purposeful. There are plenty of dysfunctional people in the world who have no qualms about subordinating others for their own gain, who are unmoved by suffering and think nothing of the consequences of their actions. Their motivations do not extend beyond themselves. They are not, in my book, Purposeful. They may, however, be effective. Many of the organizations and leaders in the world whose actions have catastrophic impacts on people and the planet are highly effective in their domain. There are also Purposeful people who oppose them and make it their life's work to do so.

I am a great believer in Buckminster Fuller's philosophy that "You can never change things by fighting. You have to create something new which makes the existing reality obsolete." My choice is to give myself to the creation of ways and means by which people can realize their glowing, abundant magnificence for themselves, within themselves. And I wonder... what would a world be like where there is a critical mass of people passionately living their Purpose on a daily basis?

As mentioned earlier, a critical mass is an amount of fissile material needed to create a chain reaction. In other words, the amount of people who need to be living their Purpose committedly to generate a chain reaction in people so that it becomes the norm.

A few years ago I ran a series of workshops with one of the world's leading organizations. The brief was to help them live their values on a daily basis. The company's values were Passion, Integrity, Leadership, Ownership and Trust. The principle of the workshop was: nobody has a monopoly on human values. Passion for one person might be dancing on the table with a rose between their teeth, while for another it might be sitting in a squashy armchair with a great book. Neither one is better than the other and it is oppressive for an organization to say to its employees "thou shalt be this form of passion and no other". As a result, the workshops were focused on helping people explore these values on a daily basis in all that they did so that they were infused in their language, behaviours and mindset. To kick-start the process of exploring passion I brought someone in to teach African drumming. Never having done any drumming before, the group found it hard to hold the complex rhythms so we did an experiment with critical mass. We made sure that three of the group could hold the rhythm. When they did, the remaining 25 people easily managed to consistently hold it. Three people for that group was critical mass. Imagine then a critical mass of people beating the drum of Purpose, passionately and unstoppably giving the contribution they find most compelling – what would the world be like? What might change?

We would solve the major problems facing the planet... clean drinking water, a balanced ecosystem, oceans clear of plastic and petrochemicals, clean and abundant food, the fundamentals of life for all people, mass evolution of education, unlimited free clean energy, the end of human trafficking, non-violent resolution of problems, another level of dynamic cooperation across borders, industries and peoples, a United Nations that works for the benefit of all, politicians who are truly representative of the people and with the humility to serve, corporations which give back, health industries committed to self-healing, television programmes and films which work to the highest common denominator of intelligence, the confluence of arts and sciences, and truly globally collaborative projects such as space exploration, to name but a few. A critical mass of Purpose-driven people on this planet would change it beyond recognition. Newspapers would be inspiring, kids would love their schooling, we would as a species move beyond survival into "thrival".

I like that picture. I'm not sure if it's accurate, but I know that it's good. Hundreds of millions of people asking themselves, every day, "What's the highest possibility?" can only bring good things. That's what I'm in it for. That's why I do what I do, why I created the Seven Questions System and why I wrote this book. I would like you to discover the immortal, unstoppable wellspring of inspiration and adventurous unfolding inside yourself. I would like you to join with others so that that inspiration combusts and catalyses itself. I would like you to take any or all of my vision, and my ideas and those of others who hold to a higher truth than the status quo, and enhance them a thousandfold with your own flavour and signature. Nobody has a monopoly on possibility.

When we live our Purpose different strands of our life fall into place. Our horses start to pull together and we discover a new level of will, commitment and engagement. It is not a cure-all. There are always challenges to overcome. Having Purpose does not make life easy, but it does make it meaningful.

There is a famous story of Gandhi working in the fields. A woman approaches him with her son.

"Gandiji, Gandiji, could you please tell my son to stop eating so many sweets."

He looks at the woman and the boy and says, "Come back in two weeks' time."

She dutifully leaves and comes back a fortnight later.

"Gandiji, Gandiji, can you please ask my son to stop eating so many sweets."

He kneels down next to the boy and says, "Don't eat so many sweets."

"Is that all you're going to say?" asks the woman.

"Yes," says Gandhi.

"Why, then, did you ask me to go away and come back two weeks later?"

"Because," replies Gandhi, "two weeks ago, I was eating sugar."

As we know, he famously said, "We must become the changes we see in the world."

We cannot change the whole world, we can only change our world.

Let's step into the new...

Thank you.

WATKINS

Sharing Wisdom Since
1893

The story of Watkins dates back to 1893, when the scholar of esotericism John Watkins founded a bookshop, inspired by the lament of his friend and teacher Madame Blavatsky that there was nowhere in London to buy books on mysticism, occultism or metaphysics. That moment marked the birth of Watkins, soon to become the home of many of the leading lights of spiritual literature, including Carl Jung, Rudolf Steiner, Alice Bailey and Chögyam Trungpa.

Today, the passion at Watkins Publishing for vigorous questioning is still resolute. Our wide-ranging and stimulating list reflects the development of spiritual thinking and new science over the past 120 years. We remain at the cutting edge, committed to publishing books that change lives.

DISCOVER MORE . . .

Read our blog

Watch and listen to
our authors in action

Sign up to
our mailing list

JOIN IN THE CONVERSATION

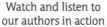 WatkinsPublishing    @watkinswisdom

 watkinsbooks    watkinswisdom    watkins-media

Our books celebrate conscious, passionate, wise and happy living.
Be part of the community by visiting

www.watkinspublishing.com